# TABLE OF CONTENTS

- Acknowledgments
- Introduction
- Growing Pains: How Can I Become More Like Jesus?
    - Activating Our Christ Relationship
    - The Soil of Our Hearts
- Finding God in the Difficult Places: The Struggle to Get Through The Pain Life Presents Us With
    - Suffering Through Pain
    - Strongholds and Vices
    - Power in Being Present
    - How We as Christians Can Impact the World
    - Are You Wearing a Mask?
    - What Comes Out of Your Mouth is What is in Your Heart
    - Pray Before You Leap
    - Imagining the Possibilities
    - Integrity
    - Humility
    - Servant's Heart
    - Servants for Christ
    - Ambassadorship
    - Our Calling
    - Workmanship
    - Patience
    - Purpose
    - Dwelling on the Past: How Does This Affect Your Future?
    - Having a Balanced Life
    - Integrity in Personal and Business Relationships
    - Letting Go of Worry
    - Turning The Pressures of Life Into Empowerment
    - Capacity for Risks
    - Meditating on the Wrong Things

- Aligning Your Life With God's Plan
- Waiting!
- Drawing Courage From Our Trials
- How God Sees Us
- Continued Pruning
- God Moves in Mysterious Ways
- Holy Spirit
- Treasure in Christ
- Fighting Back
- Being Satisfied
- Stay Focused
- Gratefulness
- Facing Life
- Gifts we Give in Relationships
  - The Gift of Acceptance
  - The Gift of Consequences
  - The Gift of Love
- Attitude!
  - Thankfulness
  - Attitude of Fortitude
  - Victory is Mine
  - Moving Forward Through Faith
- Reconciliation and Acceptance
  - Forgiveness is a Gift From God
  - Rationalizing Sin
  - Where Do I Start
  - The Potter's Wheel
  - Solitude
  - Sacrifice
- Finding Hope When All Seems Lost
  - When Things Seem Hopeless: What Now?
  - What Causes Us to Lose Hope?
  - Losing Hope When Our Expectations Go Unmet
  - Stepping Into God's Promise
- Conclusion
- References
- Other Books By This Author

# Acknowledgments

I want to thank God for the inspiration, talent, and skills He has blessed me with so I could write this book. I want to thank my family, extended family, and friends who have supported me through the years and encouraged my passion for writing. I am incredibly grateful and appreciate all of you so much!

Your decision to purchase and read my book is more than a transaction. It is a validation of my work and a testament to the power of storytelling. Writing is a part of who I am, and your support has been a driving force in my life journey. I have been inspired by the children I worked with for over 17 years, and your readership has further fueled my passion for storytelling. Your interest in my work and your feedback have been invaluable. I hope my stories inspire you to do your best, strive for success, and remember that it is not where you start but where you finish. Your support has made this book possible and inspired me to continue writing and sharing my stories because I believe in the transformative power of storytelling.

Susan M. Magras-Edwards

# Introduction

For years, I struggled with mental health issues, most likely beginning in my early teens when I lost my dad and felt that no one loved me or cared about how I felt or dealt with these issues. In those days, no one talked about mental health, and suicide and thoughts about self-harm were either discouraged or shoved under the table as just teenage nonsense. Unfortunately, as time passed, I saw myself as not pretty or too fat and struggled with my self-image. By the time I was in my early twenties, I had struggled with symptoms of Bulimia and was throwing up after many meals as the guilt washed over me because I had eaten. I went through this phase well into my late twenties, eventually deciding to give up on trying to stay slim and look like what I felt society expected of me. This strategy led to my overeating, losing self-control, and finding solace in food. This behavior has led to my yo-yo dieting, trying everything to have my cake and eat it too, and failing miserably as I sought and sometimes still seek to gain society's approval and expectations of how I should look and feel. These many years of overindulgence have led to my becoming severely obese and dealing with kidney disease, high cholesterol, and borderline diabetes that I now face.

While the struggle with mental health can be blamed on many things, what I put in my mouth is my decision. I am constantly working through inner thoughts and my negative relationship with food. I pray for self-control always, and on occasion, I am successful, but for those of you struggling as I do, you are not alone in your journey. Our society doesn't help when all the right foods and good things for your long-term health are expensive. It is no wonder that so many of us struggle with our relationship with food. When you live on a budget and work multiple jobs to make ends meet, eating on the run and not finding the time to exercise the minimum required thirty minutes daily, five days a week becomes another challenge. It also doesn't help when you get older, and no matter what exercise you do or how much less food you eat, the weight does not want to come off. Also, if you can lose weight inevitably, something causes you to pause or reduce your efforts that helped you to lose that in the first place. I cannot tell you how frustrated I often feel about this.

Society tends to praise and focus on those who are slim and sexy, as well as those who are beautiful, so for those of us who are just your average Joe or Jane, the feelings of being less are difficult to get rid of. It is time to fight against these images that only slim people are beautiful. A person can be attractive at various stages in life, and it should not matter what we look like. Too many people are judgmental and inconsiderate of the feelings of others in our society and have encouraged this negative behavior for far too long.

I don't know about others, but I have struggled with my self-image as an adult and felt like a failure for a long time. I often wondered why so many others succeeded in their careers, yet despite all my education and experience, I couldn't make any headway. I would get into my headspace and couldn't get the negativity out. Getting into my headspace leads to negative thinking and ultimately to self-harm thinking. As a society, we often want to brush aside these feelings and lack of self-worth, but it is time to address the struggles that so many face regularly. I am not saying I am depressed every day, but what I am saying is that I struggle with it enough to believe that I need to look at ways to curve this negative thinking. I am not big on medicating unless your mental health has become life-threatening. For me, turning to God in prayer works. The other thing I am working on is self-forgiveness and forgiving others. The saying is true that forgiveness is more for us than for them. When we carry around unforgiveness, it becomes a burden for us, and often, the other person is unaware that they offended you, did something wrong, or doesn't care. It is high time we begin forgiving ourselves and others and moving on. If we continue to dwell on all the bad things we feel others have done to us or focus on all our flaws, it will be difficult for us to ever reach an actual place of peace in our lives.

This book addresses many topics and highlights some of my struggles. I hope it will encourage you to address the issues in your life and find ways to embrace self-care to live the kind of life God intended for you. I apply biblical principles to my life and use God's Word to find encouragement daily.

## The LORD Is My Shepherd

**A Psalm of David.**

**Psalm 23**

¹ The LORD is my shepherd; I shall not want.
² He makes me lie down in green pastures.
   He leads me beside still waters.
³ He restores my soul.
   He leads me in paths of righteousness
   for his name's sake.
⁴ Even though I walk through the valley of the
   shadow of death,
   I will fear no evil,
   for you are with me;
   your rod and your staff,
   they comfort me.
⁵ You prepare a table before me
   in the presence of my enemies;
   you anoint my head with oil;
   my cup overflows.
⁶ Surely goodness and mercy shall follow me
   all the days of my life,
   and I shall dwell in the house of the LORD
   forever.

# Growing Pains: How Can I Become More Like Jesus?

## *Activating Our Christ Relationship*

When you plant a seed, one of the first things to be established is not the stem but the roots. Without the roots, the plant cannot grow and be strong. Similarly, it is like planting a seed when we accept and follow Christ. We need Him as the root to strengthen us so we can grow strong in Him. However, this does not happen if we accept Him and do nothing else. Following Him is much more complicated and requires action to establish and grow a strong relationship with Him.

First, we must become active in our faith through prayer, worship, and service. By doing these things, we begin to establish roots in Christ. As our relationship grows with Him, our roots get stronger, and we can stand up against opposition when it comes. If our relationship with him is passive or superficial, we fall over at the first sign of trouble when all hell breaks loose because our roots are not established in Him.

Our relationship with Him cannot be casual or happen once weekly on Saturdays or Sundays. We must take time to talk to and acknowledge Him daily. By constantly contacting Him, we can understand His desires for our lives.

(Reference: Colossians 2:6-7)

## *The Soil of Our Hearts*

Remember that your heart is like a garden; what you sow there is what you will reap. We should strive to sow good seeds through our thoughts, ideas, and attitudes. When we have stinking thinking, have evil in our hearts, or walk around with a bad attitude, it reflects on the outside and is what the world sees. Stinking thinking creates hard, rocky soil in our hearts. Weeds begin to grow there and soon take over any good seeds that may have been sown and growing.

Allowing this to happen changes the kindness, love, good attitude, and joy that may have once resided in our hearts. We must go through the process of weeding and clearing out all the bad things we have allowed in.

If you already have a heart overgrown with the weeds of negativity, please know it is possible to change your heart to a clean and pure one. I have been here at this place, and while it has been a challenge, God is restoring my heart. We cannot hope to change the condition of our hearts by ourselves. We need God's intervention in our lives. All we need to do is give up control and let Him get to work.

I don't want a rocky, shallow, and thorny heart. I want healthy soil, which I tend to do regularly. Just like our gardens outside need weeding, fertilizing, watering, and nurturing, we, too, need God to come into our lives and clean out the messes we have created or allowed to creep in.

(Reference: Luke 8:4-15 – the parable about the Sower)

# Finding God in the Difficult Places: The Struggle to Get Through The Pain Life Presents Us With

## *Suffering Through Pain*

Eight years ago, I found myself amid an emotional crisis. I am sure that although it seemed to occur overnight, it had been building for a long time and just hit me at that moment. It got so bad that as time went on, I believed in my head and heart that God had honestly forgotten me and my life would soon be over, possibly by my own hands.

I would drive home in my car with tears streaming down my face. I would cry to God, "Where are you, God?" The pain was all over me, and I struggled to accept that I could not handle these emotions of anger, frustration, sadness, hopelessness, disappointment, and bitterness on my own. I have been a control freak most of my life, so relinquishing control of my life's direction was and, in some ways, still is challenging. I was mad at the world, others, myself, and God. I wanted to blame everything and everyone for what I was going through. My struggles resulted from my pride, selfishness, and unwillingness to believe I could not care for myself.

I was scared and confused, worried that my life would never feel normal again. I was on a roller-coaster ride I hated and could not get up the courage to jump off. I cried almost every day, and while most people who knew me never saw it, the pain was there in the shadows, haunting me daily. I was in denial about my life's tailspin, and I couldn't admit I was wrong and needed help to get off this crazy ride.

It took talking to my closest friends and family, delving further into God's word, and simply facing my problems head-on for me to come out of the miry pit. It took bowing before God, confessing my sins, and admitting I was wrong and needed His help. Then, the long process of healing began. No, I am not out of the woods yet; however, I can feel and see the changes in my life. There are times when I fail miserably, and frankly, my heart breaks when this happens because I again feel like a failure despite knowing that I have come a long way from where I started.

I am sharing all this with you because I know I am not the only one who has struggled emotionally and spiritually, and if I can help but one person, then I will have made a difference. Man or woman, it matters not; all of us struggle through different things in our lives. Despite our difficulties and challenges, there is always an outlet, always a solution to our temporary seasons. Please do not make a permanent decision due to a temporary problem. It may all seem hopeless, but in the end, God will make it right. We all can overcome the pain and sorrows that life hands us. You cannot fix these problems alone, nor can I. I tried to do it on my own but failed miserably. I don't want you to beat your head against a brick wall thinking I am man or woman enough to handle it alone.

I didn't want to admit I struggled because people tend to judge us. Sometimes, they do not understand what we are going through but are willing and ready to judge and criticize. This reality is sad because people struggling with stress, depression, disappointment, heartache, and loss need to be comforted. They need to know they have someone who cares enough to listen without judgment and confidently do so. We don't need people pretending to want to help us but then gossiping about us, spreading our business, or lying about us on the streets.

God hates gossip, so let me lay that right there for you to think about and consider. Are you a gossip? Are you taking what is already a struggle for someone and compounding it by gossiping? I know I have had to consider this in my own life. Stop gossiping in its tracks, and you will do someone an excellent service.

If you are struggling today, I encourage you to write it down, say it, and admit you are broken and need help. In our brokenness, we open a path for obedience. Being an emotional wreck for most of my life was not ideal, but I learned it is okay to say that I don't have everything together. It is OK to say you need some intervention to save your sanity. We all need Jesus now. We can't wait until we have it all together to reach out to God and say, "Where are you, God? I need help." I learned this the hard way; frankly, the hard knocks of life and poor decision-making results are not the route to take. Take it from me, whose stubbornness and self-serving attitude resulted in situations I could have avoided.

God is wise, has power, and can bring us peace that surpasses all understanding. He comes to us amid our pain and helps us get past the pretense and the barriers we have erected in our lives. When going through difficulties, we tend to create and erect barriers as a self-defense mechanism to protect ourselves. When we go to God in our pain, He can tear those barriers down and transform our lives for good.

He gives grace to those who humble themselves before Him and resists pride. Giving up control of our lives is challenging, yet when we are willing to do so for God, He can help us cope with whatever life throws our way. Jesus tells us we are his disciples if we abide by his word. And you shall know the truth, and the truth shall set you free.

(Reference: John 8: 31-32)

When we are honest with ourselves and Christ, He can see us through our life's journey. It may not always be easy to obey the Lord, but it will all be worth it. Just imagine what He will do for you when you remain faithful and obedient. (References: Psalms 51:6 and James 4:6)

## *Strongholds and Vices*

We sometimes have strongholds and vices that keep us from a close connection and relationship with God. For some people, it's rap music, smoking, social drinking, binge eating, comfort foods, television, pornography, bad relationships, etc. For me, it has been the comfort foods and binge eating. When my emotions are wrecked, I become an emotional eater. I turn to food as a coping mechanism to deal with the various challenges in my life. Of course, this is not good because food should be for the sustenance and nutrition of our bodies. We should not use food to console our emotional highs and lows. The Bible talks about gluttony; I feel this falls into that category. Proverbs 23:20-21 – "Be not among winebibbers; among riotous eaters of flesh: For the drunkard and the glutton shall come to poverty: and drowsiness shall clothe a man with rags." Other verses in the bible talk about uncontrolled eating and drinking. I don't drink alcohol, so that has never concerned me. I do, however, love food, especially sweet desserts, so I must not allow food to continue to be a source of comfort in my times of trial.

The things we see and hear eventually infiltrate our minds and hearts; thus, we must be careful what we allow to enter us. We should do our best to be selective about what movies we watch and the music we listen to regularly. Our culture is saturated with films and music filled with violence, people cursing, talking about killing, and looking down on women as objects. I am not saying people should not be able to make money; I am saying it should not be at the expense of others or to the detriment of specific individuals in our society. Since this is something we cannot control, it is up to us to determine what will harm our minds, hearts, and souls and work to eliminate or, at the very least, minimize how often we interact with these things.

We might say to ourselves that it's nothing, but we have become desensitized to our society's criminal acts and moral conduct. With all those things competing for our attention, it is hard to hear God's voice and allow Him to shape our thinking, perspective, and worldview. If we are not careful before long, the world will shape our viewpoint, and we will place our faith in it and not in the word of God.

God wants continued fellowship with us, so we must guard our minds and hearts against the things of the world that threaten to separate us from Him. I like knowing God is ready and willing to stand in the gap for me. I like knowing He has my back no matter what I am going through. God is the ruler of our lives, so we should honor and glorify His name. He is not finished with us yet. I am going to celebrate what He is doing in my life. I will continuously work on having an unbroken fellowship with Him.

(Reference: Romans 6:10-12 and Proverbs 10:22

## *Power in Being Present*

I mentioned before that sometimes we need to know that someone cares and is willing to listen to us without judgment. Knowing someone is there with you, listening, not saying much, and holding you through your pain can make all the difference in the world. There is power in being present through someone's trials and difficulties. We are often so focused on our agendas that we cannot see past them to notice that someone else is in pain or suffering and needs our help. Ask yourself if you are making yourself available to add value, strength, and encouragement to the lives of others. Let someone know that you are there for them. Not to offer your opinion, fix their problems, heal them, or make them right, but to be a good listener and hug them.

There is humility in being present. We don't have all the answers, for only God does. All we need to do is show up, bring a meal, and sit quietly with them. Facing challenges in our lives is a process that only God can get us through and facing them alone can be difficult. I realize we are never truly alone if we have God in our lives, but it is always nice to have someone care about us and offer a hug of comfort as we go through the process. God is the only savior, and what happens in our life is up to Him. Our role is to help a person feel safe in our presence and be an active listener as they share their deepest thoughts and feelings without us going out and breaking their trust. In several commercials, they say, "What happens in Vegas stays in Vegas." Our pastor says, "What happens in the small group stays in a small group." (Pastor Hennie Bosman, The Rock Church, Temecula, CA) We must apply those same principles when someone trusts us when speaking confidentially.

We shape our lives by the choices we make and our actions. We should consider whether the choices we are making and the steps we are taking are impacting the lives of others. Become a better listener and strive only to advise if asked. Even when asked, give advice lovingly. Our job is to get to know people and to learn to engage with them on the same level. None of us is better than someone else or worse than they are. We are all walking along the path, trying to reach Jesus. He died on the cross to bear our sins, not just a chosen few. Offer your friendship to someone in need. God loves us so much; we should learn to love each other.

(Reference: John 15:9-12)

## *How We as Christians Can Impact the World*

Studies show that approximately 2.2 billion people are Christians. This number represents about thirty percent of the population. Imagine if we all decided to permeate our culture and communities with kindness, love, and grace. People would come to know the Lord and begin to follow the ways of Jesus. It's like the yeast in the dough described in Matthew 13:32. Imagine our impact on those who are lost, broken, discouraged, and experiencing feelings of hopelessness. Together with God, we can create change.

When I listen to politicians talk about change, I don't hear them discussing the kind of change I am referring to. The Ten Commandments give us directions and instructions for living our lives if only each of us could live by those rules. What a difference that would make for all of us in the world. By the very existence of the Ten Commandments, we are connected to the justice system we have in place today. Consider, if you will, how crime, hate, and abuse would be reduced if we followed those ten principles set forth by God.

(Reference Mark 12:28-31 and John 1:1-5)

## *Are You Wearing a Mask?*

People wear masks not just at Halloween, for health reasons, or a masquerade party. On those occasions, they wear them as part of their costumes, but for the rest of the year, many wear an invisible internal or external mask to hide their insecurities, fear, and weaknesses. We believe the lies the enemy tells us about ourselves rather than dealing with them head-on. These masks represent our defensive mechanism, which we use to cover up our misery.

Several individuals in the Bible believed they were not good enough, yet they overcame obstacles in God's power and through His redeeming grace. For example, people like Gideon and Moses saw only their weaknesses, while God saw their potential.

Sometimes, we allow our insecurities, weaknesses, faults, and beliefs about ourselves to take control of our lives, which leaves us immobilized with fear. We become stressed out and begin to believe the lies the enemy keeps telling us. We must wrest back the spirits of prosperity and joy from the enemy's hands. Remember that John 10:10 says, "The thief comes only to steal and kill and destroy; I have come that they may have life and have it to the full." He is there to steal our joy, kill our hope, and destroy our dreams, thus creating havoc in our lives if we allow him to.

Fear is a stealer of joy; it kills our hope, destroys our dreams, and keeps us from realizing our full potential and all the benefits and blessings God has for our lives. I don't know about you, but I don't want the enemy camping out in my life. I might appear to others to be weak, as Gideon appeared in the Bible, but through Christ, who strengthens me, I can overcome fear and withstand the enemy's assaults and attempts to overtake my life.

We are children of God, and once we acknowledge this and understand our true identity, we can become mighty warriors against the enemy, the one God designed and ordained us to be. God loves you. Do not allow your insecurities to hold you back. Ask yourself what insecurities may be holding you back and begin to address those. I have struggled with this, so it is difficult to ask anyone, much less ourselves.

Start developing 'possibility thinking' to strip away the phony masks you hide behind. Reveal your true identity and revel in the thought that as adopted children of God, he empowers us to greatness for His name's sake.

(Reference: Judge 6:1-40 and Psalm 139:14)

## *What Comes Out of Your Mouth is What is in Your Heart*

For a very long time, my son Justin kept telling me that my thinking was negative and that I needed to work on my attitude. Frankly, I was bitter and mad at the world for all the failures I had experienced and was not happy with myself or my situation. He was right, although I initially didn't want to believe or accept it. Then I started paying attention to what I was thinking and what was coming out of my mouth, and I realized it was not very nice. If I am honest, I still have those moments, although not as often, and I fall back into this negative thinking ever so slightly in my weakness. The enemy is always on patrol, aware of those weaknesses, and will use them at every opportunity against us. We really have to be careful what we say out into the atmosphere. Our words are more powerful than we think.

When we are thinking negatively, then we speak negatively. The thing is that what we speak out of our mouths, God can hear, and I honestly think it affects our entire persona as well as our potential. I say this from experience: I am not judging you, but I want to let you know I understand. I have been there, and it has become a daily practice to be conscious of what I am saying and thinking. Sometimes, I lose it and forget everything I have learned, and in my frustration, I allow hurt feelings and misunderstandings to get in the way of positive thinking. We must learn to stop spewing negative nonsense out of our mouths. When we speak all that negativity, it creates an atmosphere that is not conducive to growth. It's like we take in all these negative vibes; the next thing you know, it's like having a puke/vomit blown into your face. Your life becomes one big mess. When you are struggling with these challenges, it makes it difficult for others to understand what's going on with you, and they often don't want to be around you because you cannot control your thoughts or emotions.

Likewise, if we speak positive and good things into the atmosphere, we receive them back. Remember that God spoke the universe into existence. Therefore, when we say good and positive things into the atmosphere, God breathes life into them and turns the impossible into possibilities.

We must believe that miracles will happen if Jesus speaks into our situation. Matthew Chapter 8 talks about the centurion's story. Take some time to read it. We must change our mindset and our attitude. I want Jesus to speak into my life and say, "Let it be." I wish that the things I pray for in my prayer closet, on my knees, and in my time with Him will come to fruition because Jesus says so.

Believe! Believe that the things you desire are possible through Jesus Christ. When the centurion spoke with Jesus about his servant, he believed Jesus could heal him from where He was. Jesus responded in Matthew 8:13, "As you have believed, so let it be done for you." We have not, not because we haven't asked, but because we believe not. I know some of you may not understand that, but take it from me when I say that my lack of faith in God has hindered me more than my belief in Him.

We must learn to control the negative thinking in our lives and to control our tongues. Our speech dictates much of our lives, and the struggle is real for me. It's not so much about gossip but negativity and feeling sorry for myself. I have also been the kind of person who shoots from the hips and asks questions later. This attitude and behavior are not always good, mainly when dealing with our loved ones and close friends. While learning to control the temptation to act this way, I have continued to struggle with the behavior and asked God to intercede on my behalf. Nothing is wrong with being honest about our feelings or thoughts, but how we share them should be considered beforehand. As my husband tells me, think long and hard before sending that email or text, especially when upset. My weakness and identity struggles have allowed the enemy to overpower and affect my life through my lack of self-worth. We must fight our internal battles daily before hoping to win the raging war on the outside. Put your game face on and step out in faith. Take hold of your future by embracing Christ and the love, mercy, grace, and abundance He has prepared for you.

(Reference: Matthew 10:15-Judgement, Matthew 8:1-13 – Centurion, James 3:8-10 –The tongue, and Ephesians 4:29 – Corrupt words)

## *Pray Before You Leap!*

When following our dreams, many of us become paralyzed with fear. Fear of failure, fear of the word "no," fear that people won't like us, or fear that people will talk about us or criticize what we are doing. For example, when giving a speech for the first time, your hands go clammy, your mouth gets super dry (this happens to me at job interviews), and you become nauseated or feel butterflies. Your mind may go blank as you try to remember what you want to say, and well, it just doesn't quite come out the way you planned it, no matter what. Even when I have had notes, it never goes how I planned it out, and I often wonder why I bothered to prepare because I just blundered the whole thing. If you are anything like me, this causes frustration, and sometimes you may even call yourself names because you are so mad at yourself for messing things up.

I have learned that we must pray to God in every situation. I have found that I fall behind when I try to go ahead full steam without first consulting with God. Sometimes, we seek to make a significant life decision and only see one available option. Before you plunge into the pool with both feet first, make sure that option is viable and makes good common sense. I cannot tell you how many times in my life I leaped first, then turned to God to ask His advice instead of vice versa. Trust me when I say I have landed myself in deep water more than I care to admit. You reap what you sow; boy, have I experienced the fallout of hasty decisions.

When a significant decision weighs on my heart, I sweat, and stress grows inside me. So, I always try to pray when anxiety begins to sneak into my life. Rather than panic, I am sitting down, praying to God to gain His counsel on the situation. Far too often, we are in a big hurry, and we don't stop to think through the problem and look at the big picture. We allow ourselves to be influenced by others or factors unimportant to the decision. We worry about other people's opinions when, unless the decision affects them somehow, it should not matter. Their opinion of me is none of my business!

I am naturally a worrier, but I want to reduce that tendency and change my attitude and behavior. I have committed to immediately praying when worry or fear creeps in. Praying gets my mind off my situation and focuses on God. Pray changes my perspective, helps reduce my stress, and opens my mind to what God wants to reveal.

The expression "look before leaping" is good advice. You never know what you will be stepping into or on when you jump unquestioningly into a situation. We must evaluate all aspects of a problem, including our plans and life visions. Consider the big picture and seek counsel from God and those with experience or knowledge that could help you decide. Again, I don't always follow through, but I believe I will get a handle on this with God's guidance, time, and patience.

When it comes to following our dreams, we should consider whether this is what God has planned for our lives. If your plan is not aligned with God's plan, you are setting yourself up for failure. Even if you see some success, without God in the picture controlling your destiny, you will not see your full and true potential. Don't get me wrong; I am not telling you not to follow your dreams, as that would be stupid. I am saying to stop and ask God questions before deciding. Don't allow yourself to receive pressure from outside sources. They are just distractions meant to deter you from making a wise decision.

Since many want what we want, we rarely consider the far-reaching consequences of our decisions or actions. I am not saying to be indecisive about following your dreams; I am saying go for it, but remember that when you go out there, you will face obstacles and individuals who do not want you to be successful in your endeavors. Matthew 10:16 tells us, "Behold; I send you forth as sheep amid wolves be ye therefore wise as serpents, and harmless as doves." That means we need the strength and security that Jesus provides us.

Have faith and believe in the impossible, but don't take dumb risks. Seek counsel and understand all of the options and risks you will encounter. Find a quiet place to meditate on what's ahead and allow God to open your mind to receive new information, opportunities, ideas, and cautionary words that He may have for you. Ask Him to open the right doors and guide you in the right direction. Don't be hasty in your decisions because you think you have to do everything now. I believe God makes us sometimes wait for reasons we may not always know or understand. I have learned over the years that if you "Act in haste, you will repent in leisure." (This is credited to William Congreve but believed to have been a saying before his writings in 1962) I have lived and experienced this to my regret. Not every idea or vision you have is the right one. Make sure your plan is feasible and that God blesses it.

Everything we desire to accomplish in life requires planning and preparation. Don't try to drive past this part of your dream. This part is the most frustrating and time-consuming for some of us, but it is essential to your success. Even athletes must plan and prepare, often for many years, before participating in the Olympics. Sometimes, they do all that work just to run in one race. The same thing is true when following our dreams. Occasionally, we will spend many years planning and preparing just for that one opportunity. Make sure you are ready because great opportunities rarely come knocking twice. Les Brown has said in one of his motivational tapes that "It is better to be prepared for an opportunity and not have one than to have an opportunity and not be prepared."

(Les Brown, You Deserve Motivational Speech, he adopted this saying from Whitney Young, Jr., to whom it is credited initially) I am ready when God opens a door of opportunity for me. Are you prepared?

(Reference: 1 Peter 1:1-13 - Gird up your loins and Exodus 4:1-9 - Moses)

## *Imagining the Possibilities*

We all have the power to imagine. As we age, our ability to imagine diminishes for some of us. We begin to accept that things are the way they are and that nothing can be done about it. I beg to differ and honestly believe that we can revive our imagination and our ability to envision God's possibilities. We have mental blocks in our lives that limit our possibilities. These come about because of our life experiences, mainly when those have been negative.

God wants us to begin imagining great things and step out in faith, believing in the possibilities. Imagine Abraham when God asked him to go to another place. He was stepping into the unknown. He didn't even know this place existed but trusted God to see him through.

In our obedience, God opens doors of possibilities that allow us to move forward in our lives. Don't live in the past or get stuck in the present. Too many of us dwell on the past so much that we are paralyzed with fear and cannot move forward. This is a real struggle that when we are there, we must fight it. The same applies if you are stuck in the present. I know that I have struggled with both. I have made so many mistakes in the past and have often dwelled on those. I also feel stuck in the present because of my current situation. Helen Keller once said, "Security is mostly a superstition. It does not exist in nature, nor do the children of men as a whole experience it. Avoiding danger is no safer in the long run than outright exposure. Life is either a daring adventure or nothing." When we think that we are secure, we are not. Life is fragile, and at any moment, our time may come. We live in fear of the past, our present situation, and the unknown of the future. We allow fear to immobilize us if we are unwilling to take a chance.

Far too often, we fear the "What ifs" in life. How about we begin thinking about all the things that can go right? Let us focus on the possibilities and begin to live our purpose. I, for one, am tired of being stuck in a rut. We must start imagining ourselves as the winners God wants us to be. Limit the fears you allow to creep in. I struggle daily with this, but I am working to improve at keeping those fears at bay. For twenty years, I had so many rejections and failures that I could make a book with all the job rejection letters alone. How can I move forward if I continue to sit here and feel sorry for myself? God meant for us to be mobile, so sitting still is not helping us.

Psalm 56:3 says, "When I am afraid, I trust you." Too many people are unable to move past their previous failures. We cannot continue to allow our past to dictate our future. God says to forget our past. He is not sitting around focusing on our history. His focus is on our future, where He wants us to be. None of us have a sterling resume or clean background. Look, for instance, at some of the great leaders in the bible: Peter, Abraham, and David. I mean, they were not all that wonderful. Like the sailor he was, Peter cursed, Abraham tried to give his wife away twice, and David was an adulterer and murderer. God didn't give up on them, and He won't give up on us either.

God cares about where we are heading, not where we have come from. I often told my students, particularly those struggling in life and with their schoolwork, that it is not where you start but where you finish. Our pastor, Hennie Bosman (The Rock Church Temecula Valley, www.gotrock.org), said, "God made our bodies facing forward. He placed our eyes facing forward so we could see moving forward. He put our ears facing forward so we cannot hear what people say behind our backs. Our hands are facing forward, and our feet face forward so we can walk in faith. The only thing in the back is our behind. Why? Because some things are best left behind." I love listening to his messages as they inspire me to want to do better. He does not mince words and references everything from God's word.

God calls us to have the imagination to live the life He called us to live. Living and walking in faith allows us to live beyond the physical and mental limits that exist in our lives. Allow the Holy Spirit to reshape your imagination.

(Reference Ephesians 3:20, Mark 9:23, and 2 Corinthians 12:9-10)

Take your limitations in stride. We must have faith that helps us to rise above our limitations. Through Him, we can do the impossible. Allow God to build you up. Don't allow the enemy to tear you down. We should be demonstrating God's kingdom here on earth. The Lord's Prayer says, "On Earth as it is in Heaven," so I question why we are not living our lives that way. He gives us possibilities, so we should be demonstrating the opportunities God has for us.

Do you want to write a book? How about starting your blog? Do you want to create and start a business from home and are too scared to take the chance? We must be willing to step out in faith and take reasonable risks if we can hope to achieve what God has planned for us. Les Brown said, "We have to be sick and tired of being sick and tired." He has also stated many ideas and dreams are buried in graveyards because people talked themselves out of pursuing them. (Les Brown, You Deserve Motivational Speech, credited originally to Fannie Lou Hamer, 1964) Those individuals allowed themselves to be overcome with fear and let that hold them back from achieving what God planned for their lives. I don't want that to happen to me. I am pursuing my dream of being a successful writer, blogger, proofreader, and editor. It is more

challenging than I imagined, but I keep plugging away because if I stop, then I will let the enemy win.

Let us stop being short-sighted about life. We are always moving towards the eternal. It's like running a marathon. The scenery constantly changes, and you will face many ups and downs as you move through life. Life is not intended to be a sprint, so slow down and fight the good fight of faith. God wants to do something in your life. Remember, we can have all the hope we desire, but hope is not a strategy. Faith with works is a strategy. Now get up, get moving, and let's believe God together that we will achieve the impossible through Jesus Christ, who strengthens us.

We do not deny our mess; we acknowledge it but will not roll over and play dead. We will not play around with our lives but will grasp them and take hold of God's possibilities. We must become a kingdom man or woman doing the King's business. Are you doing the King's business today?

## *Integrity*

We must ask ourselves what integrity means to us. How can we foster integrity in our lives? What can we do to please God and live with integrity and honesty? (Reference: Proverbs 11:3-5) We should strive daily to glorify God. Everything that we do in life should bring glory to Him. Our commitment to living with integrity and honesty should extend to how we work, conduct ourselves at home, act at church, and behave within our community. We can glorify God in multiple ways.

For example:

- Conducting our work in ways that please Him
- Showing ourselves with the right attitude, words, and actions
- Treating people with respect
- Treating people fairly
- Valuing others: they are essential, too
- Use your position or status to glorify God by advancing morality and righteousness.
- Acknowledge that he is the actual owner of your business, but not only that, he owns everything and is the Lord of everything.

Everything we do must please Him. It is the only way to glorify Him. Ask yourself why you are doing what you do and whether it is for God's ultimate glory. If not, what can you do to change it? What does glorifying God look like? I must stop and make sure I am not acting in an unethical way in business. If I must use unscrupulous practices to make my business successful, I am in business for the wrong reasons. If I am in business and God is at the helm, then unethical practices should never enter in. (Reference: I Corinthians 10: 31 and I Chronicles 16: 28)

## *Humility*

"Pride comes before a fall." (Reference Proverbs Chapter 16) We have all heard this or something similar said when we fail to humble ourselves and show humility. Pride is not all bad, as there is such a thing as good, healthy pride. Good pride is that feeling of self-satisfaction and self-respect when we have accomplished something. Unhealthy pride is to think more highly of ourselves. We believe we are better than others or put our needs above others because we deserve better treatment. Unhealthy pride also includes valuing ourselves more than we do others around us. I am not saying we should not love ourselves, but I am saying that we should not think that others are less than we are because we have more, know more, or do more. We are all called to different purposes in life; with that said, some of us will have capabilities that others may not. That does not make us better than others.

When I think of unhealthy pride, I think of those historical fictions I loved to read where the "ton" in England was the place to be in years gone by. Ordinary folks had no actual worth in the eyes of this society. For members of the "ton," the elite did not associate with the lower classes as they were beneath them. The most a commoner could expect in life was to be a servant in the elite household in society. The same thing happens today, not just among the wealthy and privileged but also among all classes. We encounter this attitude, even among people experiencing poverty, simply because some believe they are better than others for multiple reasons other than money, class, or power. I use historical fiction as a reference to make a point about unhealthy pride, so please don't take offense; none is intended.

When we walk humbly with God and rely on Him for everything, we can learn to avoid prideful attitudes. When we stray from God and do not seek Him out, we are more likely to succumb to the temptation to act with an overabundance of negative pride. Be an example of healthy pride. God honors us when we humbly serve, putting Him and others before ourselves. Give glory and walk humbly, staying focused on Him. Remember to have a servant's heart.

(Reference: James 4:10 and Micah 6:8)

Humility was hard for me and still can be a challenge. It stinks, but I have realized the blessings that come to me through stronger relationships because of God's changes in me. When we act with too much pride, we tend to drive others away because of our bad attitude. Who wants to be around someone who thinks only of themself or thinks they are better than everyone else? I have found that when you seek to be humble, it is far better than having your pride crushed. When we intentionally seek to be humble, it brings along more pleasures in life. We should actively seek humility, turning our minds away from prideful thinking.

Even Jesus humbled himself before God and sought to take on the form of a servant. Going to the cross and dying there was a form of the greatest act of humility. He died for you and me in one of the most humiliating and horrible forms of death. Not one of us would have been able to handle the treatment Jesus received on our behalf.

Remember that God is the King of the universe. Everything was created by Him and for His glory. Nothing that we have truly belongs to us. Jesus is humility incarnate. He said, "I did not come to be served, but to serve." Wow! I want to be just like Him in my attitude.

I have learned that I am sometimes wrong. I have learned that I do not always have to be correct. I always ask myself if it will cost me a relationship that means a lot to me. Does it matter if I am right or not? It is tough when we know we are doing things behind the scenes, but someone else gets all the credit or recognition. It might make us want to scream that our hard work resulted in their success. The thing is, that person knows they are wrong, and you know you are right. Does it matter in the overall big picture? God has our backs, and even when someone thinks they have gotten over on us, God's got it all under control.

We must rise above the temptation to let our pride take over. Please do not compare yourself to others; it rarely ends well for you or them. We do not need to compare ourselves to others to feel better. Trust in God and believe in yourself, knowing you are adopted into his family. God has his plans for your life. In Jeremiah 29:11, God tells us, "For I know the plans I have for you, plans to prosper you, and not harm you, plans to give you hope and a future." Remember this when you struggle to compare yourself to others, where they are in life, and what they have achieved that you have not. Your turn is coming; just give it time.

Do not allow pride to grow in the soil of your soul. Once it takes hold, it is tough to uproot. Just think about when trying to remove certain weeds from your garden. Sometimes, you must take extra steps to dig them from the ground. If you do not treat them with some weed treatment, they will grow back.

For this reason, the best thing to do is not let these weeds of pride take hold of our lives. Remember that it is by His grace that we are who we are. Nothing you do can be accomplished without Him. He knows, long before you acknowledge it, what you will or will not do in your life. By His grace, our hearts are changed.

We can approach relationships with new life and hope and build upon them, not because we earned grace or deserve it, but because God ordains it. Jesus died to save us, so humble yourself as Jesus did. Actively pursue humility and receive it as a gift of God's grace.

(Reference: I Corinthians 4:8-17, Philippians 2: 3-8, and John 13: 13-17)

## *Servant's Heart*

God expects us to have a servant's heart and attitude. Be inspired to serve others without expectations of something in return. Too many of us do things for others, but we expect something in return for our time, service, money, or sharing of our knowledge and talent. In John 13, Jesus shows us how to have a servant's heart. Be an example of what having a servant's heart looks like. Do not be picky about whom you will serve. We are called to serve everyone, not just those who we like. We should model for others what being a servant to others is all about. We should try to embody a servant's attitude in everything we do.

(Reference: Philippians 2:7)

Jesus tells us that success is not through position, power, or authority but heartfelt service to others. *(Reference: Matthew 20: 26-27)* We will succeed in all we do when we walk humbly in the footsteps of our Lord and Savior, Jesus Christ.

How can you encourage others to have a service attitude? What are some ways we can specifically demonstrate a regular attitude of service? Are you being a model employee? One who is a servant to your co-workers?

(Reference: John 13: 3-5, John 13: 12-17, and Philippians 2:5-7)

## *Servants of Christ*

We must think of ourselves as servants of Christ, just as Paul tells us to in Corinthians. Many of us face an identity crisis because we have forgotten who we are. Most of us identify ourselves by our jobs, titles, positions, or places in society, but those do not describe us. Our true identity is that we are children of God. He adopted us into his family to be loved and welcomed by Him. God declares us as righteous. He gives us gifts of grace and mercy. He does this not because we have earned or deserve it but because of what Jesus did when he sacrificed his life on the cross. He purchased your sins when he did this; we are worthy of God because of Him.

When we think of servants, we think of the lowly societal positions where someone is master and lord over someone else. We might think of mansions and rich people who have others cleaning, cooking, and waiting on them. It is not the type of service or servant's heart God calls us to when he asks us to be humble and serve others.

Christ is the Lord of our service. Whatever we do for others should please Him. We are stewards of the talents or gifts God has blessed us with, and they should be used to glorify Him. We must seek not to develop a judgmental attitude like the Corinthians once did. Remember that God is the one who ultimately examines and judges us.

Judgment is complex at best, and it makes us uncomfortable under the scrutiny of others. It is not our place to judge others, although many of us fall prey to the temptation to judge others based on any number of guiding opinions or thoughts. Most of us experience relationship difficulties because we develop a judgmental attitude. Many challenges and failures in relationships directly result from judgment and pride. When we begin to think more highly of ourselves or act selfishly towards others, we fall into the trap of pridefulness, which never ends well.

God's grace is the only way and reason why we can dig ourselves out of the dark hole that pridefulness drops us into. When God opens our eyes to bad behavior, he allows us to see relationships differently. I should know because, in my relationship with my husband, I have seen a vast improvement in our attitudes toward each other as we have had a revelation about how we were behaving. God defuses your judgmental attitude and air superiority over others through subtle or even drastic changes, depending on what is needed in your life. He bestows humility upon you, one of the best gifts you can receive. It changes your life. I should know because he has done it for me.

(Reference: I Corinthians 1-7)

## *Ambassadorship*

Ambassadorship is a full-time job. Our subconscious actions also reflect who we are as Christians. Those private moments say more about us than our public persona and intentional ministry. The Holy Spirit resides in us. Through the Holy Spirit, God transforms us, making us more Christ-like. When others see our gradual transformation, they can then begin to understand what God can do in their lives. It is why we must live like Christ every day. I don't think we realize how closely people watch and observe us. We are often clueless about the secret evaluations and assessments of others. When you tell people you are a Christian, they immediately assess you. I don't believe they are looking for good qualities; they are trying to find cracks in your personality and behavior. When you mess up, they wait in the wings to criticize you for calling yourself a Christian but behaving or saying things a certain way. We must commit to following Christ seriously; otherwise, the people around us will not take us seriously.

(Reference: Romans 12:18, 2 Corinthians 3:12-18, and 2 Corinthians 4:1-6

## *Our Calling*

The call of Jesus is for all sinners; that's you and me. The ministry of Jesus is to reconcile all sinners to God. All believers are called to act as ambassadors. Believers are set apart by their assignments. We have received gifts, talents, abilities, experiences, circumstances, and opportunities to work together for God's purpose. God uses us to further his message and accomplish his purpose. We begin to understand God's purpose for us when we realize that no one else can do what we do quite like us. When we experience a sense of fulfillment, we do what we were designed to do. God assigns each of us a niche, which becomes our area of ministry. Some people mistakenly believe that means what we do in church; however, I genuinely believe that our ministry/niche is wherever God places us, including in the workplace.

God equips us for whatever he calls us to do. You were created with God's purpose in mind. Ephesians 2:10 tells us, "You are God's workmanship." I am, and you are a product of God's vision. He decided what we could and should be. His vision needs to be made into reality. Too many try to help or limit God by putting him in a box. If God has called you to do something, he will lead you to it and equip you with the skills, knowledge, and materials you need to accomplish it. Paul said we are crafted to do good works. The works that God has for us are important and are different from those of someone else. Knowing that God has something in mind for us is incredible and exciting. Don't give up before God reveals his plan for your life. He has something particular for each of us, according to Paul. We have no right to live visionless lives. If God has a vision for us, we should do something with it. Everything we do towards fulfilling our purpose is part of the bigger plan of God.

God put everything we are purposed to do into motion long ago, even before birth. Our vision comes from God and is rooted in the past. When we act on our vision, we make lasting impacts that will last an eternity. Try to discern your purpose. Ask God to align your purpose with his will and purpose for your life.

## *Workmanship*

*Ephesians 2:10:* "For we are his workmanship, created in Christ Jesus unto good works, which God hath before ordained that we should walk in them." You never know when God will call you to do something that will significantly impact the lives of others. Perhaps you are already following your calling or your purpose. In Lord of the Rings, Galadriel states, "Even the smallest person can change the course of the future." Why can't that person be you? We must be willing to step out in faith to embody and fulfill God's purpose. We do not have to be fully equipped with the knowledge, strength, or ability to achieve God's will to be a willing vessel and allow Him to work through us. Humility and a willingness to accept the Call of Jesus in our lives are keys to our success in fulfilling our purpose. His will is perfected in us, and he uses us to do the great things he desires. God uses the smallest, most humble, and least noticed people to do great things. Are you willing to accept His challenge? I want to be highly favored by God. Are you ready to surrender your life to Him? There are no prerequisites to answering God's call or fulfilling your purpose. We don't need to know how to speak well (Look at Moses), be great orators, or have many skills for God to use us.

(References: Luke 1:30-37, John 1:46, Luke 1:42, and Luke 1:38)

## *Patience*

Patience is one of my most significant weaknesses, and I don't know about you; I hate to wait for anything. Waiting in long lines, waiting for a job, waiting for my weight loss to be successful, you name it, I don't like it one bit. The reality is that sometimes, we must wait. Trying to take action before planning and preparation are complete could spell disaster. I should know because it has happened to me more than I care to count. God works in us to prepare us for His vision and plan. He knows what lies ahead, so He prepares us for the future. God is sovereign. Remember that if we act hastily or foolishly, we will mess up. Don't allow a sense of urgency to cause you to make regrettable mistakes. I have certainly been there, and it is a bitter pill to swallow when facing the consequences of your mistakes. This is particularly true when those mistakes could have been avoided. Although waiting makes us anxious and impatient, it is essential to wait on God. Remember that our visions are simply an extension of God's vision. His timing is perfect.

God works on us until we are ready to act on His purposes. Everything He does is according to His timetable, not ours. (I need to keep reminding myself of this.) Once the vision of God is clear, we are usually ready to jump into action. Knowing the vision will not prepare us or ensure we are ready to act. Don't be impatient! I realize it is hard for most of us to hear or understand, but we must let God lead the way. Put Him at the helm and step back. I mentioned this to my husband, who told me I might need to go in the passenger seat instead of the driver's seat. He knows that when I get excited about something, I want to forge ahead without waiting for God to tell me it is okay to act. I didn't take it personally because it is true. Now, I won't promise I might not become a backseat driver, but at least from the back, I cannot try to wrestle the steering wheel from Him. We all need to accept the training He has for us. Remember that vision precedes preparation. (Reference: Colossians 1:9-14) God is preparing you and me for the work He has for us. Look at how he is already preparing you to fulfill your vision effectively later on.

(Reference: Philippians 2:13)

## *Purpose*

What is my purpose? Many of us have asked God and ourselves that question for some time now. I have often said I want to fulfill God's purpose for my life, but I have no real idea what that is. If you are like me, you have probably thought the same thing and asked this question countless times without getting any closer to the answer you seek. I am passionate about writing, and words come to me faster than they do for others. So, am I supposed to be a writer? I don't know, but I will pursue it until God says otherwise.

We often hear others talk about purpose, but do we know and understand what that means? Our purpose should be combined with our identity. If our identity is that of an adopted child of God, then our purpose should be ordained by Him. Paul wrote that we are God's workmanship. He designed each of us for a specific purpose within His kingdom. He has called us all to do something meaningful and wonderful to make a difference. You matter and are essential to Him. He is there when you feel stuck in a rut or like life is passing. When illness hits, or challenges arise, remember that God loves you. Focus on Him and not on your circumstances.

While I realize that may be easier said than done (I can relate), do it! When God places something in your heart, and you cannot seem to let it go, think about it. Are you called to it? Does it inspire you to want to do more? When your identity is grounded in God, and you trust Him, he will become a part of your vision and reveal

His purpose for your life. He will provide the necessary skills and tools to fulfill your purpose. He has written an excellent purpose for your life; as you pursue it, you will begin living your best life in Him.

(Reference: Ephesians 2:10)

Many want to make a difference, leave their mark, or impact lives. However, we often fail to achieve this because we do not take on the mantle of the Holy Spirit. We need to allow the amplifying power of the Holy Spirit to work through us. We must take a leap of faith and go! I know this is something I need to embrace. When doubt creeps in, it becomes difficult to see how the power of the Holy Spirit can empower us to higher heights. We cannot act alone. We will also never get anywhere if we stand still. God is waiting for us to move. Stay calm about how it will all work out. When we act in faith, God strengthens us and sees us through. Hebrews 11:33-34 talks about the power of God helping normal individuals, like us, do extraordinary things. We do not accomplish what we do on our own steam, through our skills, by our level of intelligence. By God's power and spirit, we finish our tasks successfully. We accomplish these things through faith in Christ.

(Reference: Matthew 22:36-39)

We must start small. Unfortunately, many of us want to move from point "A" to "Z," and we forget all the work to be accomplished in between before we can reach the end. It's our impatience rearing its ugly head. We want things to happen overnight, which will not occur in reality. Trying to take on something too big, too quickly, and without God's direction creates countless problems, and we get in over our heads. Find something that has been laid on your heart. Start small and work your way up. I believe that seeking small successes and more challenging tasks is better. I am not saying you should not dream big or limit God. He is limitless, and there is nothing too big for Him. If you want to share God's Word, do not start with a large crowd; that might be too overwhelming, not to mention you will encounter more critics right out of the chute. Start with close family and friends. Share your faith and remember to be an example of what it means to be Christ-like. Timing is everything. Be sure to gauge when you will share with someone, knowing they may not be receptive to what you say. I believe Christ wins over some people through their behaviors and actions rather than what they say. You can talk to some people until you are blue in the face, and it will not be until they see fundamental changes in you that they begin to wonder what is different about you and how they, too, can enjoy what you have. Be patient. Yes, I know saying that is easier said than done. Believe me, I struggle with the temptation to lose my patience often.

You should always seek God's counsel and allow the Holy Spirit to guide you through your challenges. Do not act on impulse; that rarely ever results in success. Before long, you will realize you are making an impact in the lives of others and on the Kingdom of God. Guess what? You will be doing what you were always meant to do.

(Reference: Luke17:6)

## *Dwelling on the Past: How Does This Affect Your Future?*

The rearview mirror is small for a reason. It is in the past and only poses to remind us of what has transpired. It tells us that we should only look behind us to ensure we do not dwell on our past. Many of us, including me, have spent too much time dwelling on past hurts, experiences, mistakes, and history. It does not matter what has happened; the past is there to show us what not to do in the future. This very idea has been coming into my mind for a long time. I have struggled with the past more than I care to share, and it reminds me of all the unforgiveness I must get rid of in my life. I have slowly been working on it, and I look forward to the future with great hope, trust, and faith in Christ.

The front view mirror and windshield show us what a brilliant future we have. They represent God's promises and that He is more significant than any situation we may encounter. It is big because it means there are numerous possibilities available to us. God is always with us and has opened our doors for a bright and prosperous future. We must take His hand and cross the bridge. We must trust Him, look forward, and step into His will, calling, and blessings.

## *Having a Balanced Life*

Having a well-balanced life is essential to our well-being. How we live and respond to our circumstances indicates how well we navigate life. You must ask yourself whether you want to have a productive and fulfilling life or if you want to allow the difficulties, trials, and negative things to dictate your emotions and the quality of your life.

Throughout our lives, we encounter many challenges, deal with multiple situations, and often lose our sense of direction as we become mired in the messiness we have allowed to become a part of who we are. We must be vigilant, as the devil does not sleep. He is constantly on the prowl and will have no problems eating you up and spitting you out. 1 Peter 5:8 tells us all about what the devil seeks to do. We must exercise caution and not allow him to sneak into our hearts and minds.

When we live a balanced life, it will help guard us against the enemy. You can only focus on work, family, or business. We must seek God's guidance in all areas of our lives. He is first, your spouse and children are second, your extended family is third, and your job and friends come next. Everything else in life falls in line after these. When God is the foundation of your life, it is far easier to handle crises than when you try to go through them on your own. I know, as I have wanted to do it on my own before, even while professing to be a Christian and a Christ-follower. It is easy to be fooled into thinking we can do things without God. Having a solid relationship with Him is crucial, and everything else falls into place.

Be consistent in your prayer life. Attend church regularly, spend time building and strengthening your relationships, and leave work at the office. Please do not make it a habit to always bring work home. Occasionally, it is okay, but as I can tell you from experience, it is challenging to stop once you get into the habit of bringing work home. It also gives the impression and sets the expectation with your employer that you should take work home and that it is okay for them to continue to load on more work. Allowing this behavior to creep into your life takes valuable time away from your family, God, and friends. Be cautious about what levels of expectations you set for your employer. I am not saying do not do your job; you should give your employer 100% of your time during the hours they pay you for. Unfortunately, many employers expect far too much from employees. Employers want you to work longer hours with no extra pay or compensation. I do not believe that God expects us to go above and beyond to the point that others take advantage of us.

When troubles begin to brew in your life, seek God first. Many of us sit and worry about the future and focus too much on our circumstances, thus taking our eyes off God. I tell you everything from my experiences and know that worry does not change or improve any situation. It does not add a single minute to your life and is unhealthy. Do not allow yourself to get onto an emotional roller coaster. Trust me when I say it is tough to get off once that happens. You can become an emotional wreck, and no one, including you, can understand what is happening. I became an emotional basket case and stayed on that roller coaster for over seven years. I contemplated suicide during those struggles. I thought that this would be the end-all to my problems. I did not think further about it because I believed that would be the ultimate slap to God's face. That would be like saying to Him, "I don't trust you, and I don't believe in you; your Word does not hold any power." I honestly never thought I was going to get off the emotional ride. My life, mindset, and attitude changed when I decided not to live like that anymore. I talked to myself, the Holy Spirit spoke to me, and the enemy tried to convince me of the opposite. On the outside, I looked fine, but on the inside, I was a big, hot mess! I asked God to empower me to break the bondage and hold the enemy had over me. I asked Him to clean out the negative thoughts, self-doubt, and trash I had allowed into my heart. This is a challenge, so do not feel overwhelmed when you struggle because the enemy will not give up without a fight.

If you are struggling today, ask the Holy Spirit to empower you and help keep you focused so you can build a life worthy of your calling. (Reference: Ephesian 4:1 and 1 Peter 5:8)

Have you considered what your life would be like without Christ? Think about how that might make you feel. The answer to that question is one of the most important. God's gift of grace should remind you and me of our lives without Him. God wants us to have a close relationship with Him. The closer I draw to Him, the more inner peace I feel.

When we develop our relationship with God, this extends to our relationships with others. The more we grow our relationship with Him, the more comfortable we feel building our relationships with others.

My question to you is, how are you approaching your relationships? Are you hesitant to start or build a new one due to past hurts? Are you dealing with trust issues because someone else caused you to lose trust in others? I have certainly been to this place!

Relationships can be challenging and complex, particularly when experiencing inner trust, anger, or hate struggles. When they work, however, this can bring us such great joy. God's gift of grace can radically change your relationship. Paul writes in I Corinthians to the Church of Corinth, addressing relationships, divisions, quarrels, and disunity. You will find this list in the first four chapters.

Sometimes, we become very judgmental in relationships and think more highly of ourselves. Our pride also gets in the way of strengthening relationships with others. Pride causes divisions and quarrels. We must be aware of this and exercise caution lest it causes us to stumble or fall. We were all in the same place before Christ came into our lives. Let us not allow our selfish thoughts or wants to overtake our good judgment. *(Reference: 1 Corinthians 3: 1-23)*

We must watch that our carnal nature does not become a big part of our identity.

## Integrity in Personal and Business Relationships

Be a person of integrity. Be a person of good character. Be a person that is above reproach. Integrity guides us to do what is right in our relationships with others. If we follow God's truth, His guidance will follow us daily with clear instructions and bring peace to our souls. When you do what is right, you can look at yourself in the mirror and sleep well at night, knowing you have done the right thing. (Reference: Proverbs 11:3) I have struggled to sleep at night, and my conscience has bothered me when I have not been sincere or come clean for inappropriate actions.

Some people might prosper over you by being dishonest and crooked in their business conduct; however, God does not sleep or slumber and will honor and bless you for doing what is right. One day, they will have to count the costs for the errors of their ways. Do not allow yourself to fall into a trap of dishonesty to move your business forward. Your good character will one day catch up to you in blessings just as their character will catch up to them in curses. Do not compromise your integrity in relationships, whether they are personal or business.

One day, we will all have to answer to God for our conduct. Do you want to face our heavenly father and explain your behavior to Him? I would instead meet Him with my excellent character rather than a deceitful one. I am not perfect; only God is perfect, so I must account for my attitude and behavior towards others and God daily.

When doing things in life, many of us do not like others telling us what to do, mainly when their point of view differs from ours. My husband likes to say that if people stopped to look at the big picture and count the costs, their decisions in life might be very different. He also says that many of us think the things we do in secret will remain there. We fail to realize that just like when you shine a light into a dark basement and the rats and roaches scatter, so will the light reveal what we have hidden in secret. None of us lives in a vacuum, so whatever we do in secret will become known and ultimately affect those around us. Never think, for once, that what you are doing will only hurt you. It hurts everyone else around you. We do not always consider that our decisions are not made in a bubble, as we do not live in one. Your choices, good or bad, affect you, your family, and sometimes your friends. I certainly made some decisions earlier in life that I wish I could go back and change. At the time, I did not think of the consequences of those decisions or the effect they would have on my family.

When we conduct ourselves with integrity and are true to God's word, he provides us peace of heart and mind. We receive priceless blessings from God. It does not mean we will not face adversity or encounter trials, but we will certainly avoid the eternal consequences of not living an honest life. When we profess to be Christians but live in an ungodly or dishonest way, lacking integrity, we do great harm to the cause of God. When we live right in our lives and relationships, God is glorified.

## *Letting Go of Worry*

The devil uses worry to manipulate us, take away our self-control, and draw us away from God. God tells us in Philippians 4:6 that "We are to be anxious for nothing." Worry creates anxiety, stress, and even illness if we allow it to go on for too long. Worry keeps us from acting and moving forward in our daily tasks and lives. Worry is a trust issue we have with God. Ask yourself whether you trust God or not. Either you do, or you do not. Believe in God's promises to you. Remember, He said He would never leave us nor forsake us. We must trust in His promises so He can deliver us from worry and help us find inner peace.

(Reference: Psalm 56:3)

When you trust in God, yes, you will still feel the emotions of your circumstances. However, anxiety, stress, and fear will not be your regular companions. Who wants to be worried all the time? It does not feel good to be constantly worried. Our attitude becomes harmful when we are wrapped up in worry and stress. I know that is how I feel whenever I allow worrying to dominate my life.

When we worry, we open the door for the enemy to enter our lives. Do you want God's covenant promises to happen in your life? If so, choose God and trust Him. Cast all your cares upon God.

(Reference: Deuteronomy 30:19, Reference: 1 Peter 5:7-8)

Have faith in God. Trust Him with all your heart, soul, mind, body, and strength. Shut the devil up. Shut him out. Shut down his operation and his power over your life. Let God take the wheel of your life. Let Him be in charge. Make Him the driver and see just what he will do for you. (Reference: Psalms 34:4-6) Ask God to help you; do not let worry rule your life. Choose to trust Him.

(Reference: Matthew 6:27, Psalm 56:3, and Job 3:25)

## *Turning the Pressures of Life Into Empowerment*

We wrestle with our desire to regain control when we suffer through trials. As we go through those trials, we may often feel powerless to do something about our situation. We must be able to go through the difficulties life throws our way. Through these trials, we strengthen our resilience, learn, grow, and mature in our spiritual walk. Of course, it is human nature to want everything to go according to our plan, and we most often fail to accept that God is always in control, even when we believe our life is out of control. We only view our circumstances from the surface, while God looks at them from a deeper perspective.

Many believe that once we begin serving the Lord, all of life's trials will pass us by, and we will be left unscathed. Just because we believe in God, His good, and his sovereignty does not mean we are excluded from the adverse events that come our way. We will struggle just as non-Christians will, and sometimes even more than they do. When we work, we seek worldly solutions when our situation requires supernatural attention. We may regularly try to face a temporary crisis by applying permanent results. We want to resolve our problems immediately because going through trials certainly does not feel pleasant. As our Pastor, Hennie Bosman, The Rock Church Temecula (www.gotrock.org) likes to say sometimes, "We want things to happen in a microwave world, but God is in the Crockpot business." Well, something like that, but you get the picture. We want things to happen quickly and for our dire situation to disappear; however, God says, "No, I need you to walk through this right now."

Let us face it: no one likes trials and difficult circumstances. Who does? We must trust in God to walk with us through the winter seasons of our lives. The more you focus on trying to wrestle with natural solutions, the more energy you will waste. You cannot and will not learn everything God has in store for you if you continue to focus on your problems and not on Him.

From my years of suffering, I have realized that God was and still is primarily responsible for carrying out His calling in my life. You must be pruned or put through the fire to understand how you will empathize with others' suffering. The longer you refuse to relinquish yourself and your life to God, the longer you will take to come through the fire. Stubbornness and pride must be removed from your life and replaced with humility. Put your trust in Him and believe He will see you through and guide you every step of the way.

(Reference: Romans 8:28 and John 15:2)

## *Capacity for Risks*

I touched on the topic of risks and want to expand on the fact that when we put our faith in God, we trust the unknown. That, in human terms, is called taking risks. For some people, taking a risk is dangerous and can spell ruin, but for others, taking risks equals possibilities and future success. As I said, we take risks in our homes, cars, or simply crossing the street daily. Taking reasonable risks is a typical action. However, some risks require more of us and demand that we investigate them before becoming involved.

When you enter a situation blindly, the results can be devastating for you and perhaps others around you. The consequences of a blind risk can affect your life for many years and may take you a lifetime to recover. We must take measured risks that are not foolhardy, and we have sought counsel. In the end, chances are inevitable; however, when you take calculated risks that align with God's plan for your life, you can envision a successful future. More than once, I have made the mistake of entering into situations without counting the costs and have lived to regret it. In many ways, I am still paying the price for those decisions even today.

God allows us to become like seeds needing to be covered and watered to grow. Every plant or tree needs tending to, and during these difficult times, it may seem as if God has abandoned us, but in reality, he is there working on us, supporting us, and strengthening us. If God does not prune us or we do not plant the seeds in our lives, then we will not grow. If we cannot succeed, we will never realize our full potential.

You must allow God to shift your mindset. As a former elementary educator, I always talked to my students about a growth mindset, which means changing negative thinking to positive thinking. The same mindset shift applies in our lives when we live for and focus on God. When our mindset shifts, we begin to see things from a different perspective.

We can now see that what has happened to us was orchestrated by God to help us grow. Sometimes, we are so focused on earthly things that we take our eyes off Him. Oliver Wendell Holmes, Sr., is credited with the quote, "Some people are so heavenly-minded that they are of no earthly good." When we face adversity, it is crucial to keep our focus on Him. Miracles happen, fruits spring forth, and you can now see your full potential.

Fear keeps us from fulfilling our dreams and our full potential. Please do not sit on your potential; live it! See if your faith will not grow. Begin to experience new growth and realize your future. So, do not balk at your struggles. Embrace them and thank God for enriching your lives with them. I know this is easier said than done. Believe me when I say that going through trials is no joke, and I do not feel much like praising Him when facing difficulties.

I am so glad God moved me from an old plot of land lacking nutrients and growth potential. I am pleased he chose to replant me in a new garden with richer soil filled with nutrients and more significant growth potential, my fruit-bearing field.

(Reference: John 12:24)

## *Meditating on the Wrong Things*

When going through trials, we tend to focus on our circumstances because they are causing us pain and suffering. Reflecting on all the years I wasted worrying about my troubles and circumstances, doubting God, and leaning on my own understanding, I bow my head in shame and regret, especially as I call myself a Christian. I am not wallowing in my guilt; however, because God has seen it, I am delivered from the constant worry. While I did not understand why I was going through all of that, and in some ways still going through it, I realized that it was my winter pruning season, and God was preparing me for more extraordinary things. He has released me from bondage to the enemy's hold on my life. I feel free to embrace the little moments, thus the theme of my former blog, Embracing Life. I no longer spend all my time worrying about my situation, for I trust Him. My faith in Him has grown.

For those of you going through trials, do not give up! Believe me when I say that the enemy wants to isolate you. He wants you to stop praying and to draw you away from God. He wants you to believe that no one, including God, loves you. The devil wants you to feel self-pity and identify as a failure. I know this because I have been there. God will never tell you such lies! God wants great things for us. Do not let the enemy deceive you! My son Sean is the one who reminded me of this one day while I was going through the worst depression I have ever felt. That year, he gifted me with a book by Dr. Seuss, "Oh, the Places You'll Go!" He reminded me of Paul's words to the Romans, reminding them that no one could stand against them because they were more than conquerors! I keep that close by so when I feel out of sorts, I can read his comments to me. It reminds me that I am a child of God and that he has purposed great things for my life. We all need these little reminders when our troubles seem more than we can bear.

Troubles always signal God's intent to take you to a higher level. You are in a growth process and sprouting a new life. You are on the rise. When I am trying to draw closer to God, I am reading my bible more, focusing on Him, or he is trying to take me to the next level, and all hell seems to break loose. Allow God to help you break free and break through the hard soil you have been buried under for so long. Let Him help you rise to the surface towards the possibilities He has for you.

(Reference: Jeremiah 29:11 and Psalm 119:71)

## *Aligning Your Life With God's Plan*

God designs us for a specific purpose. Only when we fulfill our purpose can we carry the load we are expected to bear. God aligns us with the purpose and calling he has for our lives. We are His workmanship and are created for His good works.

(Reference: Ephesians 2:10)

God has given us talents and spiritual gifts, which we are called upon to use for His purpose and glory. He gave us hearts filled with passion for specific things that align with our purpose. When we allow ourselves to be used for His purpose, He is glorified, and we see our most significant potential. When we try to do things independently (He gives us the freedom of choice), we cannot see our full potential and will likely fail in our endeavors. Just consider the rich young ruler in the bible. Jesus told him what he must do and let him walk away, knowing what would happen to him. God allows us to choose, so I suggest we choose wisely.

When God places a passion in our hearts, we should not sit around waiting for His next move. We need to move, and he will equip us. Sometimes, God is waiting for us to move. What are you waiting for? Step out in faith, grasp the bull by the horns, and do what God has called you to do!

## *Waiting!*

Are you as tired as I am of waiting? Do you struggle with having to wait for an answer to your prayers? If so, join the club. As I mentioned before, I hate to wait for anything. I hate waiting in lines for answers and for someone else to do something I can do faster. The list goes on and on. However, the one thing I find consistent is that God gives us His answer in His time. It does not seem to matter how important it is to us; if it is not in His will to provide us with an answer now, then it will not happen. Even worse than that is the fact that His answer might be a resounding NO! I do not know about you, but I do not like the word no, even when no is in my best interest. God gives us answers such as "no," "not now," and "yes." In other words, "No," "Grow," and "Go," as Pastor Rick Warren (Daily Hope, former senior pastor of Saddleback Church, Author of The Purpose Driven Life) has said in one of his studies I heard on KWVE radio, 107.9 FM.

Before we can accept our life's calling, we must go through a season of fermentation or growth. It is the season of waiting, growing, and being molded by God to fulfill His purpose. For us, this is the most challenging season of all. It is painful and complicated, making me break out in a cold sweat. While it is a time to develop and grow our relationship with God, it is not easy to live through. Most of us will draw closer to God when faced with this season if we focus on Him. We may ask why we are going through these difficulties, but we must go through them to gain the skills, knowledge, strength, faith, and trust in the Lord. While we are waiting, God is making something new inside of us. God works on our hearts, courage, and motives; throughout it all, He works on our wisdom. He puts us through the fire, taking out all the impurities, refining us, and developing the skills we will need to meet and complete our mission on this side of heaven.

When God feels we are ready, he will transition our lives to where he wants us to be. We will then be prepared to move on to the next season and step into the next level of His plan for us.

(Reference: Matthew 9:16-17)

## *Drawing Courage From Our Trials*

All of us have a cross to bear. As time has progressed, the cross has become a sign of hope to those who believe in Christ and the crucifixion.

(Reference: Luke 9:23 and Philippians 3:10-11)

Draw courage from the word of God. Put the promises of God on your lips the next time you face a trial. Remember when Jesus was in the Garden of Gethsemane the next time you struggle. Remember the sacrifices He made for you on the cross. When we get to the end of ourselves, we can see God perform miracles in our lives. If we are still in charge, trying to control our own lives and destiny, we do not leave room for God to do what He wills to do in our lives. Remember that God is more significant than any challenge you may face. He will work out the impossible when you come to the end of yourself. Communicate with God through prayer. Trust in His word. It would help if you were filled with the Holy Ghost. We can reach God through prayer, so do not allow yourself to lose face or forfeit God's hand. God wants to work through you and for you. Do you want the power of the Holy Spirit to lead you? Do you want God to answer prayers in your life? Ask God to come upon you and guide you. Walk with Him Daily.

(Reference: Ezekiel 37:1-10, Mark 14:32-36, Isaiah 53:1-6, Matthew 20:17-19, and Acts 2:22-24)

I want the Lord to empower me with the Holy Spirit so that I might fulfill His divine will in my life. We have so many churches in our world, yet we have no significant impact on those in our communities, our country, or the world. This is because we lack strength, influence, and life. We must ask God to lead us by His Spirit. When you find yourself in an impossible place, God is the only one who can lead you out. We must begin to claim victory. Ask the Lord to surround you and to speak into your future. Ask Him to be a buffer between you and the enemy so you can defend against the negativity that comes at you from all sides and angles.

Call on God's voice to speak into your life and drive out the fear, doubt, and unbelief in your heart. Allow God to be the ruler of your life. His promises are accurate and real.

(Reference: Acts 2:1-3, Psalm 139:23-24, and Mark 9:23)

## *How God Sees Us*

Many of us struggle with our identity because we look at ourselves from a human perspective rather than a Godly perspective. God is not looking at who or what we are at present. He is looking at who he can mold us into becoming. He does not expect us to be perfect or the best example. We are not. He is the only ideal being, and on our best days, we are still considered filthy rags in God's eyes—however, none of these matters in the overall scheme of things since He will change us anyway.

We all need the strength of God, just as the disciples needed Him in the upper room. When we allow pride to enter, we cannot see the full potential of God's blessings in our lives. The early apostles did not rely on their skills, wealth, or knowledge to witness to others. They relied on God's power, strength, and leading to move them forward in their ministry. Allow God to speak into the impossible situations in your life, for while it may seem impossible for you, nothing is impossible for God.

## *Continued Pruning*

For God to do what he wishes with our lives, He must prune the old fruit and cull them from our lives. When we experience multiple losses, we think these things are essential and irreplaceable. I am not talking about losing a loved one but about jobs, houses, cars, personal possessions, and even toxic relationships that hamper our growth in Christ. Of course, we are hurt by these losses, but ultimately, God's blessing for you and me far outweighs those losses. God secures our next season of blessings in the new harvest. Miracles happen constantly, but we are so focused on our trials that we cannot see those blessings waiting to happen or that have already happened. Instead of grieving your loss, be thankful for what God is doing. Be grateful that He brought you out of that situation.

Let me explain: I lost my last full-time job in December 2001. I had been waiting for God to deliver me to a new full-time job. I went so far as to return to college to "Reinvent" myself to secure that job. I worked part-time and full-time as a substitute teacher for over seventeen years. Several years before, I did everything from a notary public, real estate, crafter, childcare provider, and a few others to make ends meet and secure that dream career. God knows best, and obviously, none of those things has been what God had in mind for me. It has been a bitter pill to swallow, feeling like a failure and believing that God was against me through all of this. Therefore, I beg to differ with any of you if you think I do not have experience with loss and disappointment. I finally said enough is enough and left education and self-pity behind. While I enjoyed teaching and working with those exceptional children, I needed to allow God to change my direction. Writing is my passion, and I love telling stories, so here I am, writing in multiple genres and sharing with others my experiences. Has it been challenging stepping out in faith? Absolutely! I must hold on tight because I never know what God will do next, inspire me to write, or who He will send my way to work with.

I have realized that not everything we believe is right for us is approved and blessed by God. I must say that what God has taken from you and me, He did not think it was good enough for us. Why would He let us keep something or be around someone terrible for us? I believe where God is taking us in our lives is where we need to be. We do not need to take any of our baggage, yesterday's stale bread, and the weight of everything in our past with us on our journey into the future. Do not take your regrets with you; they will only keep you back, hold you down, and stop you from receiving your blessings. He only wants us to carry what we need into our future. Know that whatever happens in each season of your life, if you do not need it in the next season, God will take it from you. Some of us are hoarders and want to take everything with us.

I, for one, am becoming a minimalist. We recently made some changes in our home, and when I say that my trash bins have been full every week, I am not kidding. My husband and I decided that rather than leave all this stuff we have collected over the years to sit around gathering dust, we would rid ourselves of as much as possible. While no one wants to think about their end of life, I think about it, and really, cleaning out all these things will simplify my sons' and daughters-in-law's lives when we are gone. Less is more, and I am getting rid of all the baggage that will weigh me down on my journey. Who needs to be carrying dead weight anyway? Right?! I am carrying enough body weight around, which I am gradually working to eliminate.

My husband and I used to have an orange tree in the backyard. Not having any idea when to pick them, we let them continue to grow on the tree. One of my neighbors told me that the longer you leave them on the tree, the more time they have for the sweetness to come into them. We are like those oranges. Sometimes, God leaves us on the tree a little longer than we would like so the sweetness of our future success can come to us. He does not want us to be picked too soon because we will not be ready. Like the oranges, God wants us to have flavor and be equipped with the necessary skills and knowledge to fulfill His desires. He wants to grow us, which may mean a more extended winter season. Praise Him in all seasons and thank Him for everything.

Back to those oranges, my husband looked at the tree one day. The tree boasted tons of flowers along with the oranges. We decided to pick one, and it was delicious. We went ahead and picked the rest, and they, too, were delicious. We had fresh orange juice for weeks.

There is a season for everything; to make room for the new season, we must get the old fruit to make room for the new. God wants to remove the aging fruit in our lives to make room for the new. This is all part of the process, and some operations take time. Be patient about getting to the next season. Enjoy the current season and know that it, just like your trials and challenges, is temporary and will change into something new. We cannot bear fresh fruit if the old fruit stays on the tree and gets rotten.

(Reference: Job1:21, Matthew 27:51, John 19:23-24, John 17:20-26, and 1 Corinthians 15:3-7)

I previously mentioned that in life, we are constantly fighting a battle. It is not so much a physical battle as a mental one. The battlefield is in our minds, and we must fight as if our lives depended on it. You must realize you are in a war. You must gear up for a battle and guard yourself. Equip yourself with the right weapons to defend against powers and principalities. 2 Corinthians 10:4-6 tells us, "We use God's weapons, not worldly weapons, to knock down the strongholds of human reasoning and to destroy false arguments. We destroy every proud obstacle that keeps people from knowing God. We capture their rebellious thoughts and teach them to obey Christ. And after you have become fully obedient, we will punish everyone who remains disobedient." This war is no joke. As Christians, we face a world that no longer embraces what God stands for. We are also facing challenges from the spiritual realm.

Once you realize you are in a war, you should consider what's happening in your mind. More often than not, I have found that we are always at war with ourselves. I mentioned before that Les Brown has said that many ideas are buried in the graveyard because many of us talk ourselves out of success or of winning the battle against failure. In the war, for Christ, there is no difference. We must arm our minds against a sinful nature; to do so, we must fill our minds and hearts with God's Word. The enemy will fight dirty and keep coming after you because he doesn't like you drawing closer to God. He will send distractions, create situations, and even send people you know to disrupt your life. If you go up against the very thing keeping you from moving forward in your relationship with God, you must cut off its head. Harriet Tubman once said, "Never wound a snake; kill it." That is so true. If you don't kill it, you are allowing it to have another opportunity to strike you. The enemy is like that; if you allow him to gain a foothold in your life, he will make it difficult for you to let go.

(Reference: Romans 8:5-7)

One thing that holds many of us back is our lack of faith and the fact that we don't believe overcoming our situations will ever be possible. We need to arm ourselves with possibility thinking. 1 Peter 1:13 says, "So prepare your minds for action and exercise self-control. Put all your hope in the gracious salvation when Jesus Christ is revealed to the world." When faced with trials and tribulations, we tend to become despondent and lose hope that we will find relief from our troubles.

The first thing we do is deny we have a problem. We develop an attitude, and in our despondency, we refuse help from others; we feel guilty and ashamed; we try to disregard the pain we are feeling, and we ignore the fact that this pain just doesn't affect us, but those around us. We get angry and rebellious, and then we begin to accept things the way they are, thus making them a part of our lives rather than doing something about it. I, for one, am tired of living a mediocre life. I want the kind of life God offers and am willing to do whatever He asks me to obtain it. Jesus meets us where we are in our lives and helps us to overcome the vulnerability we may feel while raising our level of expectation by giving us hope and showing us the possibilities life has to offer us through Him.

I want the freedom God has to offer. He is the Spirit, and where the Spirit is, there is freedom. 2 Corinthians 3:16-18 tells us this. God wants to make us more like Him. In a previous message, our pastor, Hennie Bosman, said "that we must prepare our minds for action. God is inviting us to an intentional and personalized partnership with him to renovate your reality." Do you want to have a personalized relationship with God? Do you want Him to renovate your life and change your current reality for the better? We have to be willing to change with God's help. He will provide the strength that we need. He will give us the victory.

*(Reference: Isaiah 12:2)*

Don't quit! Arm your mind so you can persevere through positive thinking. You should tie your self-worth to what Jesus did for you, not what the world thinks of you. Remember that nothing we do in life happens without God's permission. Yes, He allows us free will, but I believe that when we trust Him, He will deliver us. I strive to focus on my minor victories and progress rather than my failures. If I continue to focus on my failures, I will always feel sorry for myself, and I am letting the enemy win. Don't let the enemy win in your life. God has something great in store for you and me. When you find yourself losing faith or hope, read Hebrews 12:3-4. We are not strong by ourselves; we need God. As I have said, my life verse is: "Be strong and courageous. Do not be afraid or terrified because of them, for the LORD your God goes with you; he will never leave or forsake you."

God wants us to be happy in Him. We can find peace and comfort in Him no matter what we face. Hugs!

## *God Moves in Mysterious Ways*

God sometimes does what appears to be the strangest things in our eyes, so much so that it leaves us in awe of what He can do. I cannot tell you how often God has worked in mysterious ways and brought me through or delivered me from a situation I never thought I would get out of. I have found that God appears in some of the strangest places and during circumstances, we cannot believe He entered into. We often forget God's power and majesty and that He is in everything. What seems to be a surprise to us was ordained by

Him from the beginning. We were just being too human and looking at things from our tiny perspective while God was working in the spiritual realm, making big things happen in mighty ways.

He loves to give us good gifts and, as such, loves to surprise us in situations where we may have thought that He had forgotten us. We are not an afterthought to Him. We must learn to remain faithful even during our trials. Surprisingly, you never know when God will choose that it is your opportunity or moment to bless you. He can make us smile in ways no one else can.

(Reference: Matthew 28:1-9 and John 20:14-18)

## *Holy Spirit*

We need the Holy Spirit, and our lives must be filled with prayer and faithfulness for God to work. Suppose we live a prayerless and faithless life. In that case, we will continue to complain and lament about our inability to deal with our impossible situations, our powerlessness against the enemy, and waste our breath preaching to the masses. As I mentioned, God loves to give good gifts, but how do we experience or receive those blessings if we fail to ask and have faith that He will deliver us? When we continue to try to handle things in the natural sense, God cannot move in our lives in the supernatural.

God is in the business of impossible miracles. Give Him a chance to transform your impossible situations into possibilities. We are not alone. He is our friend and is with us always. As Carter Conlon states in his book, It's Time to Pray, "We don't need a new plan, we don't need a new superstar; we need the Holy Spirit."

(Reference: Luke 11:13)

Note: You can find Mr. Conlon's book on Amazon by following the link:

https://www.amazon.com/Its-Time-Pray-Changes-Everything

## *Treasure in Christ*

Do you ever feel abandoned by God? How about feeling beaten down, beaten up, run-down, crushed, or destroyed? Does your life ever feel like it is in ruin? Perhaps you are feeling these things right now. I know I have certainly felt that way. I described it to my family as a rock along an ocean shore where the waves beat on me daily. Every time I tried to catch my breath, the water would rapidly come in and hit me again. I felt desperate, confused, overwhelmed, and even defeated. I felt as though I were drowning in the stress, the grief, the sorrow of what my life had become in my own eyes.

What I have found, however, is that as I began to trust God more with my life, he has moved more through it. He has been helping me pick up the shattered pieces, fixing them back together in a new way as He moves along. God has seen the buried and hidden treasures in my life and me. If one looks past all my faults, sins, and bad attitude, He sees the real me buried deep within all that mess.

God is in the Rebound Business!

## *Fighting Back*

Life is full of challenges, and with technology, those challenges are compounded as people hide their true identity, personality, and emotions behind the façade they display on social media. Most of us cannot handle rejection and the problems of life that come at us from all directions. We constantly feel as though we are in a fight for our survival. People are vicious to others, and we often get knocked down by those we trusted to uplift us. Some people get knocked down so often; eventually, they cannot or will not get up. They give up on life. It's like in a boxing match when one of the boxers goes down for the count and cannot or will not get up.

Don't allow life's challenges to knock you down and count you out. Get up! Stand up! Fight back! Les Brown has a statement he makes that goes something like this: "When life knocks you down, remember that if you can look up, you can get up!" God is on your side! If he is on your side, nothing this life can throw at you will hold you back and keep you down. God is in the Rebound business! He knows what to do and how to help us when life goes out of control.

(Reference: Romans 10:13)

## *Being Satisfied*

Do you often feel satisfied or dissatisfied when you think about your life and attitude? Are you constantly seeking more, never ceasing to increase your wealth, possessions, or position? Take some time to review Philippians 2, as it talks about satisfaction. We must learn to be satisfied with who we are, what we have, and where we are in life. It should not always be about a competition to see who can accumulate more things or gain a higher-level position. It's called a "rat race" for a reason. Rats climb on top of each other to get to the top. My mother-in-law used to say that you should never muddy every pool you come to because you never know when you may have to come back and drink from it. She also said we should be kind and careful when climbing the ladder. We should never seek to step on others to get to the top because when we fall, no one will reach out their hands to catch us on the way down. These are two good pieces of advice that we should keep in the back of our minds when we think about what we hope and wish to accomplish.

The more we try to compete with others in life, the more dissatisfied we become, and in some cases, the more debt we accumulate trying to keep up with others. God knew this when he gave us the tenth commandment, "Thou shall not covet the neighbors' goods." My question is, why are we killing ourselves to become wealthier and gain more property only to leave it all behind for someone else to enjoy when we pass out of this world in death? Ask yourself if you are satisfied or dissatisfied. Then, ask yourself why your answer is what it is. Meditate on the motives behind why you think or act the way you do. Are your choices creating havoc in your life or bringing peace and contentment?

(Reference: Philippians 2:8, Hebrews 12:2, and Titus 2:11-12)

## *Stay focused on God*

In considering my writing of this section, I started with Psalms 46:10: "Be still and know that I am God." This verse speaks volumes to me. I hear God saying be quiet, don't you know I am God. I am the one who created the universe and everything in it. I am the one who rules and reigns over you. I am the God who loves you. I can do all things; nothing is impossible for me. While we are waiting, we often lose sight of who God is. He is who we should focus on in good and bad seasons. We need to develop an attitude of gratitude while waiting for Him to deliver us.

Don't worry, fret, complain, whine, demand, or try to wrestle control from God. You can't win no matter how hard you try. Without God's blessings, you cannot achieve anything in life. We may think we are somehow controlling our lives because things are going well, and we appear to be making things happen. Wrong! God ordains everything we have or achieve through His will and the strength He gives us to overcome obstacles and succeed. Our talents, gifts, and the things of this world all belong to Him. We cannot do anything except through Christ, who strengthens us! Find your strength in God. Allow Him to refresh and renew you. Find joy in God, for He will give you rest.

(Reference: Psalms 46:10, Psalms 37:7, and Isaiah 40:31)

Embrace what God is doing in your life! If we don't face life's challenges with God by our side, we will never know the highest potential we could have achieved. Remember, Christ sacrificed so much for us on the cross so we can have a life and live that life to our fullest and most significant potential.

(Reference: Matthew 11:28)

## *Gratefulness*

Remember I mentioned having an attitude of gratitude? Well, guess what? Having gratitude does not come naturally to us. Does this surprise you? Feelings of self-pity, anger, and resentment are those things that come naturally to us. Grumbling, griping, murmuring, and complaining are things we do naturally. No one has to remind us about doing these things. We must work on regularly showing kindness, being grateful, and being thankful. Due to this unnatural tendency, we find it difficult not to become bitter, feel betrayed, or hang on to hurt done to us by others. How will we succeed if we remain ungrateful for the good things in life? How will we discover the goodness of God?

We must learn to appreciate all that we have. If we stop comparing ourselves to others and become thankful for who we are, we will realize we possess unique qualities that can only come from being ourselves. Rejoice and be glad that God made you who you are. He reserved unique qualities just for you. You are valuable and have become worthy in His sight. Love yourself and show your gratitude. As Kirk Franklin says in one of his songs, "Smile."

(Reference: Genesis 41:50-52)

## *Facing Life*

Have you ever been disappointed, lost hope, faced fear, and lacked faith? We all have experienced this, some more than others. As a spouse of a Navy veteran, I realized that every time my husband deployed, there was a chance he might not make it home safely. I knew that I had to place his life and the lives of the others deploying with him in the hands of God. I tried not to worry and to focus on caring for the children in our home and doing what needed to be done to keep his spirits uplifted during these challenging journeys.

When we face life on our terms, we will deal with challenges differently than if we face them with God by our side or leading the way. Our nature is to be independent and to trust in ourselves. We often don't want others to help us or get credit for our achievements.

We think more highly of ourselves. When we put our trust in God, He carries us. He delivers us from challenges and trials. He can move mountains for you. He can and does, time after time after time. He pushes you through the most difficult challenges of your life. Give God the glory. Give Him your trust. Know that He will never leave you nor forsake you. Dwell in Him always.

(Reference: Psalm 91:1-2

# Gifts We Give in Relationships

## *The Gift of Acceptance*

When people begin relationships, they often come into it with expectations the other person cannot live up to. We imagine the fairytale we had at our weddings will continue into our marriages, or we think that because we decided to live together somehow, that will strengthen our bonds and make us the most remarkable, problem-free couple on the planet. We are far from perfect; we will soon realize that our spouse or friend is far from ideal. I have learned all these years that my thinking and actions have been selfish. When my husband and I got together, I thought I would be able to change him into the man I wanted him to be. What I got instead is a man who is an independent thinker, who is very neat (This drives me crazy sometimes), is very rigid in his standards and beliefs, took some time to understand that I didn't like the toilet seat being left up, (Yes, my bottom went skinny dipping many times in the middle of the night during those early years), his favorite word is "NO." He has some ways about him that drive me crazy. Of course, I thought I was the best thing since sliced bread. I cooked for him (this was a big joke in the early years and took lots of practice and training), cleaned, cared for his every need, served him, and eventually took care of the kids and his mom, too. I figured I was entitled to him bending to my whims and wishes whenever I wanted. I had a horrible temper, and when I could not have my way, boy, he learned about it!

I have mellowed over the years and have much more self-control, but that resulted from God's Holy Spirit intervention. Believe me when I say I am far from perfect. I am not as neat as he is (that's why his neatness drives me up the wall). I hate cooking all the time, and I don't like ironing, but I will when I must. I want my house clean, but I am okay with not vacuuming more than once a week. This sometimes would drive my husband crazy, but I think everything doesn't have to be spotless all the time. We live in our homes, which should look like they are lived in, not magazine-perfect. (LOL!)

I have sometimes thought more highly of myself, mostly because I am intelligent, talented, skilled, and can do lots of things others cannot (I must watch this because it is not pleasant to think of yourself better than others as nothing you have or can do comes from you, but God). He gets the glory for all that I am today!

In recent years, I realized I must accept my husband for who God made him be. He is perfect in God's eyes, so he should be in mine. He is loving, considerate, kind, generous, and cares for others. His love language is giving to his family and caring for their needs. I focus on those things, not those that drive me up the wall. If he does something I don't like, rather than chewing him out for it, I talk to him more lovingly and explain why what he did was not okay. He may not have realized he had done something wrong to offend me. Don't assume your spouse or your friend knows. Sometimes, you have to enlighten them but don't do it by using harsh words or having a bad attitude toward them. This is not always easy, but I continue to work on it daily.

My relationship with him has grown tremendously because I no longer focus on his faults but on his good qualities and how much of a blessing he is to me. Guess what? He has seen that difference and has worked hard to please me. He is not always focusing on my faults but on my attitude and behavior changes.

I am not saying it is always easy. Of course, I am not saying to stick with someone abusing you, either. I believe many marriages and relationships that come to an end could have been saved had we not been so selfish and didn't allow our pride to get in the way. Some marriages or relationships cannot be saved, but we should try. God should be the center of all relationships and things in our life. When we accept others for how God created them, perhaps we will realize they were sent to us to compliment us. We can all begin the process of having more robust, happier relationships.

## *The Gift of Consequences*

For every action, there is a consequence. The response you receive will all depend on your actions. In some relationships, you may have someone who is using drugs, be an alcoholic, perhaps they are into pornography, they are abusive, they may not be trustworthy, or they are sexually promiscuous with others. In cases like these, there should be consequences. No one has the right to treat others in abusive ways. Some of these individuals need help and may not feel they have anywhere to turn. This does not mean you should stick around and allow them to take advantage of you. You can still love someone, but do it from afar. You can show your love by directing them to the help they need. Some people do not even think they have a problem, so they may refuse. You do not have to put up with that. I think far too many people remain in abusive relationships and face the consequences of staying with that person. Not that the person is not loved, but they need help and need to understand that you cannot continue to condone their negative behavior. Many people have had to run to protect themselves and their children from abusive individuals. In society, we are often willing to shove abuse, addiction, mental illness, and other bad behavior under the rug. We do not want others to know about our failures, the struggles we are dealing with, or the mistakes we have made. Too many people use alcohol, drugs, and abusive behavior to feel good. You are not entitled to use someone else as your punching bag because you think the way you do.

In these types of situations, we give the gift of consequences. If it means you go to jail or rehab, then that is what happens. It is not our job to judge these individuals, but we cannot and will not condone this behavior toward others. Because God has called us to love everyone, we encourage you to seek the help you deserve so that others can be free to live around you.

## *The Gift of Love*

In all relationships and life in general, we are called to love. Not to live frivolously but to love from the heart. We generously pour ourselves into others so they know and feel loved. We do not have to be married to someone to love them. We are called to love others in all types of relationships. God is a God of love. He loves unconditionally and pours Himself into every one of us who draws near to Him and asks for forgiveness. Love is a universal gift, and we show others we care when treating them with kindness, are generous, willing to work together with them, and don't judge them for their failings. None of us is perfect, so it is important to remember that in our weaknesses and through our shortcomings, God loves us. We then should love others, too.

# ATTITUDE!

## *Thankfulness*

I am thankful that I can write and pursue my passion, no matter how small it may seem in my mind. For a long time, I have struggled with why God allowed me to continue as a substitute teacher and not provide me with a full-time opportunity. I struggled with accepting that this was where God had me, and I believe He sometimes allows us to stay where we are while He works on us. I am thankful my husband had a full-time job and was paid a decent wage. I am grateful that God closed doors while I begged Him to keep them open because I thought I knew what was best for me. I didn't realize that those doors might lead to destruction in my life and harm my family. I was very bitter about it. I am thankful for friends and family, those who have stuck with me through thick and thin and did not abandon me when I could no longer offer them something. It showed me their true character. A true friend does not leave or ghost you because you can no longer do something for them, you disagree on politics, you are doing something different in life than they are right now, and they are struggling through things you don't understand. This is the time when you have their back. This is not the time to walk away. I am thankful that God knows when to remove people from your life because they were not meant to stay there forever. Some people are in your life only for a season, and when you reach the crossroads, they are not meant to continue traveling with you on your life journey. Not everyone is for you, and God will remove them when their purpose in your life is fulfilled. People are in your life to either teach you a lesson or to be a blessing.

I am thankful for a roof over my head, food in my stomach, shoes for my feet, a warm bed, a hot shower, my good health, but most importantly, for my family and friends who have stuck with me through all of it. I am thankful for the love of my husband and my children. I am so blessed to have great siblings and siblings-in-law. Thank you, God, for all you are doing in my life, uplifting me in my trials and encouraging me to walk through the fire. I know

you will be there at the end of the road to show me the new direction and path you have in store.
If you feel out of sorts, lift your voice and thank God today.

*1 Chronicle 16:34-35:* "Oh give thanks to the LORD, for he is good; for his steadfast love endures forever! ...
*1 Chronicles 29:13:* "And now we thank you, our God, and praise your glorious name."

God is always doing nice things for us. Just as we would thank someone who has done or given us something, how much more should we give thanks to Him?
We should be grateful for all we have and what will be bestowed upon us in the future. Jesus is building a home for us, and the deed of ownership is assured. We should be grateful for this and everything else. I say to you, as I say to myself, be thankful, have a heart of gratitude, and be mindful to do so every day, no matter what you face. Our eternity depends on it.

(Reference: John 14:2)

## *Attitude of Fortitude*

My God is so big, and those giants are so little. He gives me confidence, enthusiasm, passion, and courage to stand up against all the giants in my life. Age doesn't matter because we only stop living when we last breathe. God can use you, restore you, uplift, educate, and move you forward if you are alive. Focus on your goals. Determine what your mountains are and follow the Lord closely and thoroughly. Never attempt to strike out on your own. Don't hide behind your self-pity. Thank God for His encouragement. Think of the bumblebee. Scientifically, its body is way too big compared to its wings to fly. We know its body is too big, but the bee doesn't know that, so it flies even though it should not be able to do so. Just imagine if we ignored our limitations and stepped up our game. Just think of where we could go if we trust in God and have faith that He will deliver us.

(Reference: Numbers 13)

## *Victory is Mine*

Life tends to throw us curveballs and wreak havoc in our lives. None of us can escape the inevitability of trials and life challenges. All of us will leave this earth with battle scars from our experiences. I feel, however, that if we remain focused on God and stay the course in our relationship with Him, we will experience victory. Throughout the Bible, we can see many instances where faith ultimately leads to success for many of God's people. God is in the business of makeovers and re-dos. He knows how to take our messes and turn them into genuine successes. When things are not going right, turn to God; he can fix any situation, but only if you let Him drive and guide you. Let Him be in control of your life.

Sometimes, people mean harm to us, and we take it all personally, but if we sit back, meditate, and evaluate, we will see God turning what others meant for evil towards us into something good. Let us not forget what happened to Joseph in Genesis 50:20. Jesus on the cross is an excellent example of God using evil to make good. To make good on His promises to deliver us from our sins and the enemy's hands. Don't let the enemy win in your life. Wrestle back control and put it all in God's hands. In his hands, we will see and experience sweet victory.

(Reference: Ephesians 1:18-21 and Psalms 36:9)

## *Moving Forward Through Faith*

Pastor Hennie Bosman of the Rock Church Temecula defines faith as "Being fully persuaded that God is in control of the outcome of my future! And to be stubborn to see His will happen in my life, regardless of what I am going through."

My interpretation is that I believe in a being that I have yet to see, but I know He exists because of all that he is doing for me and around me. I know He is in control of my life when I put my trust in Him because while I cannot see Him, I can see the results of His influence and impact in my life. Basically, not seeing, but believing He exists.

I believe in God for blessings in my finances, health, business, and weight-loss journey. I realize that sometimes God does not always answer us, and He may even seem like He ghosted us during our every trial. I once faced a real disappointment in canceling something my husband and I were looking forward to doing. In my brokenness and disappointment, I wanted to strike out at God for not allowing this event to occur, but at the same time, I knew that there is a blessing in every disappointment.

We may not always see or understand why God allowed something to happen, but we know that He never does anything or allows anything that He feels will purposely harm us. I cried because I was so disappointed, but I realized I could not let the devil win. He wants to separate us from God and create division in our lives, and as such, we must put on the whole armor of God and fight back. We cannot allow him to win. I refuse to let the enemy win in my life.

In a message at church one Sunday, our pastor mentioned that the "highest expression of faith is to believe even when we have not seen." (Hennie Bosman, 2019) (Reference: John 20:29) Jesus tells us in John that "Blessed are those who believe without seeing."

# RECONCILIATION AND ACCEPTANCE

## *Where Are You, God?*

I struggled for years, wallowing in self-pity, wondering where God was amid my trials and struggles. When things are going great, we often abandon God or even the idea of praying, talking to Him daily, tithing, serving, and for some, they stop attending church altogether. We begin to separate ourselves from God because we think we are driving all the good in our lives and forget that He is giving us these blessings. It is because He is seeing us through the good times. We are the ones who abandon Him.

Now, turn the tables around, and when things are going badly and we cannot see our way, we are all over God, asking Him to deliver us. Where were we when things were good? In reality, we should be seeking Him in good and bad times. I feel as though I struggle more with hearing from God, feeling His love, and even believing He will deliver me during my times of trials. I cannot say that I blame God because I was not always obedient when things were good. I often wonder if we truly realize who it is we serve. God is more than deserving of our praise and worship no matter what we are going through. "Whether we are winning or losing, God is still God" (Hennie Bosman, 2019)

We must be willing to be faithful and obedient no matter what our circumstances. I believe it is only when we do this that we can truly hear from God and see the miracles He is performing in our lives.

## *Forgiveness is a Gift From God*

When God shows us grace, He gives us the gift of forgiveness. We haven't earned it or deserve it, but He gave it to us just the same. As Christians, we forgive each other not because we have goodness in our hearts but because God has forgiven us, and likewise, we should extend this to our brothers and sisters. We cannot compare our sins to those of others. Sin is sin, no matter how big or trivial it may seem. If you have committed one sin, you have committed them all. How do you compare what you have done to God's goodness? You cannot! God is infinite in His holiness, and the difference between our goodness and His is astronomical. When a person sins against you, they now owe you a debt. The same thing applies to you when you sin against someone else. When you forgive them, you release them from their debt burden. Is this an easy thing to do? No, but it is a process that you will eventually step through. God is not asking us to forget, but He is asking us to no longer dwell on it. This is especially difficult when the wound that has been created digs deep within our hearts.

Paul tells us to be kind and merciful and to forgive others as God has forgiven us. The gift of forgiveness is a powerful tool in our arsenal, and when used, we demonstrate to God that we believe He is more capable of exacting justice than we are. Do I want others to forgive me when I have done them wrong? If yes, don't you think others would like us to forgive them?

(Reference: Ephesians 4:32)

Jesus tells us in the Sermon on the Mount, "If you are offering your gifts at the altar and there you remember that your brother or sister has something against you, leave your gift there in the front of the altar. First, go and be reconciled with them, then come and offer your gifts. *(Reference: Matthew 5:23-24)* Offering a sacrifice without restitution will not reconcile you to God. He wants us to be reconciled with our brothers and sisters.

When we are struggling with this, we should communicate with God and ask Him to help us face what we have done, seek His forgiveness, and try to rebuild our fractured relationship. *(Reference: 2 Corinthians 5:18)* In the bible, even the apostle Peter approached God with a question. "Lord, how many times shall I forgive my brother or sister? Up to seven times?" *(Reference: Matthew 18:21)* Peter was funny if you ask me. He asked Jesus the question and then offered Him an answer before Jesus could reply. He was explaining as though Jesus needed his help. God does not need our help with anything; we must stop trying to help Him. If He wanted our help, I am pretty sure He would ask.

Jesus was just Peter's match. He responded in Matthew 18-22 NIV, "I tell you, not seven times, but seventy-seven times." In other words, Jesus wants us to forgive others until we lose count of how many times we have forgiven them, just as God does not keep track of how many times He has forgiven us. He does not want us to keep track. God has forgiven us countless times for our sins, so we must also forgive.

(Reference: Ephesians 4:32)

In Matthew 18:23-35, we are told the story of the servant who owed his master ten thousand talents. The master ordered him, his family, and all he possessed to be sold to repay the debt. The servant begged his master for patience and compassion; the master forgave all his debt. Then, this selfish servant found one of his fellow servants who owed him a hundred pence. Rather than forgive him as his own master had done, he ordered the servant to pay. He was so unforgiving when the servant could not pay and had him thrown into jail. When the master found out what the servant had done, he delivered him to the tormentors until he, too, should pay his debt. Imagine if he had demonstrated the same kindness and mercy his master had shown him; he would have been free. He could not find it in his heart to be forgiving; ultimately, he paid the price for his selfishness. Unfortunately, too many of us get wrapped up in what we believe is ours, and we forget to show love and kindness to others in need.

When we are born, we inherit a sinful nature. Until we are reunited with Jesus, we will struggle and stumble through our sins. As born-again Christians, we hope that eternity will be bright. So long as we follow Jesus, this will make a difference for us. With the Lord's help, we can overcome our sinful nature. It is so important that we confess our sins and repent. As a just God, He will forgive and purify us from all unrighteousness.

(Reference: 1 John 1:9)

This does not mean we should continually and purposefully sin because we know God will forgive us. To do so would be disobedient and create a hindrance to all our blessings from God. God may block the answers you seek, which creates a barrier between us and God. This leads to impossible situations where you cannot fellowship with God. Malachi 3:7 tells us that the Lord says, "Return to me, and I will return to you." God is faithful to His word and will bless us for our obedience. Do not let anything hinder you in your relationship with God. Examine your heart, clean out the toxic stuff piled up there, seek forgiveness, be obedient, and repent of your sins. Obedience brings answers to prayers, so do as God's word says.

(Reference: 1 John 3:22)

## *Rationalizing Sin*

Sometimes, we revel in sin, so much so that we cling to it, reasoning out and rationalizing in our minds why it is okay to continue doing what we are doing. We tend to make excuses for why our actions are reasonable and acceptable. We don't want to hear the reasoning of others, are not open to halting our behavior, and ultimately, it hinders answers to our prayers and blessings in our lives. Sometimes, we are so wrapped up in our sin that the only way to be shaken out of our behavior is to receive a jolt of reality from God.

This sin doesn't have to be something big, but it is a sin, no matter how big or small it may seem. The sin could be that we love money more than God, as did the young rich ruler in the bible. (Reference: Mark 10:21) Repentance is the only thing that can remedy our sinful hearts. When God reveals our sins, we repent and confess, and God promises to cleanse us from all guilt and unrighteousness. (1 John 1:9)

So, consider this: is there a cherished or un-repented sin in your life? If so, pray and ask God to forgive you.

## *Where Do I Start?*

2 Corinthians 13:5 tells us to look closely at ourselves. Test yourselves to see if you are living in the faith. You know that Jesus Christ is in you—unless you fail the test. We must change our mindset when living for God and being a Christ-follower. You must take control of what you are thinking about in your mind and change your viewpoint. All change starts with changing our thoughts. Those thoughts determine our actions and what we think about becoming a predictor of who we are and what we will become.

When we want to change our direction, behavior, and who we have become, we must start with our thinking. You must ask yourself why you think the way you do and how that thinking affects your perspective and life. Once you know how you feel, whether positive or negative, you must begin changing your thought processes. Ask yourself why you are feeling the way that you do. Are you allowing the enemy to grab your life through your thoughts? Are those thoughts negative and in no way beneficial to your future?

We must learn to align our thoughts with what God has in store for our lives. We have to realign our purpose to His purpose, knowing that He will only bless what He desires for our life: the things that align with His plans. When our mind begins to wander, and we begin thinking negatively, we must diligently replace those negative thoughts with the word of God. We must build a habit of healthy thinking so that we are always keeping our focus on God. When we take our focus off of God, and we do not get His word in our hearts and minds, we are challenged with negative thinking consistently. I don't know about you, but I did not like myself too much when all I would speak and think about were negative things. When we are doing this, sometimes we are not even aware of it. It took my sons and my husband telling me outright that

I was doing this to see my behavior and my thoughts' negativity finally.

Expelling toxic roots from our lives is no easy task. I know from experience that it can be a long process that means giving up what I want for what God desires for my life. Sometimes, the two align, but when it doesn't, we must let go so God can fix us. Toxic roots stem from negative thinking and sin in our lives. We must give God a chance to cleanse us and heal our brokenness. Going through this process means constantly pulling any weeds that may try to infiltrate the soil in your life.

To expel toxic roots, we must first recognize that they exist. Sometimes, these are lies that we believe about ourselves or God. The enemy does not play games with us. He is earnest about dividing and winning over us. He will tell us lies, trying to get us to believe that God doesn't love us, He will never forgive us, and He will never see us through the trials we are experiencing. After a while, we begin to believe these lies, and it does not matter what anyone else tells us; we believe the lies and are struggling to understand why God has left us to fend for ourselves.

I can do all things through Christ who strengthens me. I have to keep telling myself this to make it through some days. I need the strength and courage of Jesus Christ to lift me when the enemy attacks me. I need Him in my weakness, so I do not fall victim to the enemy's tactics. I refuse to allow him to win in my life. I refuse to enable toxic weeds to grow again in my heart. I choose to replace those poisonous weeds with God's word. As Pastor Hennie Bosman has said before, "Change the channel. If you have no root, you will have no shoot and bear negative fruit." I am ready to "Fix my thoughts on what is true, good, and right. Think about pure things. Think about all you can praise God for and be glad about it."

(Reference Philippians 4:8)

## The Potter's Wheel

We often don't realize that even when it feels like God is not working in our lives. He is working, but usually, it is behind the scenes. God works on us and our situation, which may take years sometimes. Being a potter is a messy business, and we do not come to God as clean and pure, so all the impurities must be removed. This takes time to accomplish. As I mentioned, we are in such a big hurry that we want everything to happen now. God takes the broken pieces of our lives and puts them back together so that we become new vessels that glorify Him. He is like the silversmith who sits at the fire, stoking the silver into the fire until it shines like glass, and he can see his image.

***The story of the Silversmith**: "And he shall sit as a refiner and purifier of silver" (Mal. 3:3). This puzzled a Bible study group. One of the members offered to learn about refining silver and inform them in their subsequent study. He visited a silversmith and watched him at work. He watched the silversmith hold a piece of silver over the fire and let it heat up. The silversmith explained that in refining silver, you must keep the silver in the middle of the fire where the flames were hottest to burn away all the impurities. The member then thought about God holding us where the fire is the most desirable to burn away our impurities. Then he thought again about the verse. **"And he shall sit as a refiner and purifier of silver**." He asked the silversmith if it was true that he had to **sit** in front of the fire and watch the process at all times. The silversmith answered that he had to sit there holding the silver and keep his eyes on it the **entire time** it was tested in the fire. It would be destroyed if the silver was* *left a moment too long in the flames. You must leave it long enough to serve the purpose but not too long as it would destroy it. The member was silent for a moment. Then, asked the silversmith, "**How do you know when silver is fully refined?**" He smiled and answered, "**Oh, that's easy — when I see my image in it**." (Author Unknown).*

The silversmith knows just how long to keep the silver over the fire. He does not keep it over the fire too long or too short, but he knows when it is just right to purify it.

Christians, when you are over the heat, remember that God has His eyes on you. He knows when you have had enough and have been refined and purified. His timing will always be just right. When you are feeling the heat of the fire, remember that God has his eye on you, and He will "**sit as a refiner and purifier,**" keeping watch until He sees His image in you. God is intimately aware of your needs and limits. He also knows just when you have had enough. At the right time, He will remove you from the fire. The results will be at the right time. In due season, you shall reap (Gal. 6:9). As Job, trust God, "Though He slays me, yet will **I trust** in him" (Job 13:15). When you are over the flames, trust Him. The results will be for your good and His glory (Rom.8:28). Whose image is on you? (Matt. 22:20). Others can also see the image of the Lord in your life (Acts 4:13). **Can the Lord and others see His image in your life?**

(Copied from https://www.silentwordministries.org/2017/10/19/the-story-of-the-silversmith/ Article written by Ted Camp, 2017

God continually works in our lives; sometimes, what we want takes longer. Not because God cannot do it but because we are not ready. We require refinement and sometimes a makeover before God can release us to fulfill His mission for our lives. We may think we are ready and even tell God to bring it on, but that does not mean we are. God knows best for our lives, and if we trust Him, we must believe He will not send us out to complete our mission, ill-equipped or unprepared to handle what is out there for us.

## *Solitude*

It's time to focus on prayer, meditation, and reading our bible. We all have busy lives and many things to accomplish daily, but we must make time for God. He should be the first thing that we think about in the morning and the last thing we think about at night. This quiet time is a time of solitude. It is a time to meditate. Matthew 6:6 says, "But when you pray, go into your room, close the door, and pray to your unseen Father. Then your Father, who sees what is done secretly, will reward you."

We need solitude to hear God's voice. In this quiet time, we can tune out the busy world and focus on Him. We must be intentional in seeking God out daily. We cannot continue to think of Him as an afterthought. I know I am guilty of doing this sometimes when I get so busy doing other time-wasting things. I lose focus and feel disconnected from my heavenly Father when this happens. When I struggle with life difficulties, this can also occur because the enemy tries his best to draw us away from God by encouraging us to do other things that do not honor and glorify God.

Make time for God today! He is worthy of our praise and worship. He is worthy of our time; after all, He woke you and me up this morning, and now is the time to be thankful, appreciative, and grateful. We are not promised tomorrow, so let's make today the day we glorify Him. Let the words of praise be on our lips as we make time for Him in our secret, quiet place.

## *Sacrifice*

Jesus paid a personal cost for our transformation to take place. He faced insurmountable obstacles, abuse, and torture so that He could save us. For us to accomplish great things in our lives, it costs us something. For many of us, it costs us everything. I recall being in college in my late 30's and early 40's. I was working on college degrees at the time. I took off several years after the children were born to raise them to an age where they were not as dependent on me as they were when they were younger. At least now they could ask for what they needed and knew how to get things out of the refrigerator. The children were still young but old enough to know that Mommy was not spending the same time with them. I had to make them a priority, along with my husband. It cost me time, money, and sleep, and almost cost me my husband. The reality is that while getting those degrees, my family and I sacrificed a great deal. That is not the same as what Jesus sacrificed, not by a stretch of one's imagination, but I think you get the picture. Anything worth having is worth the sacrifice you make. Jesus thought we were worth saving, so He sacrificed His life to save us from our sins. No matter where you are, it costs you something to be there. Either you paid a monetary price, or you paid in some other form. We always trade one thing for the other when we want something.

When we are being tested, molded, and pressed together by God, little do we realize how much He is doing good work in us, and we cannot see the blessings that will come out of our mess. Realize that God is taking that seed he placed in you so long ago and is cultivating it. As He guides you through the changing seasons of your life, know He is with you, guiding every step; you may feel the pressure of this transformation, but God will make new wine with you at the end of the day.

(Reference: Matthew 26:39, Luke 22:44, and Hebrews 12*:1-2)*

# FINDING HOPE WHEN ALL SEEMS LOST

## *When Things Seem Hopeless: What Now?*

I don't know about you, but I have had many days when all seems hopeless, and despite my prayers, obedience, and request at God's throne, things remain the same, and my prayers appear to go unanswered. In those dark moments, I have felt like giving up because, in my head, I think, well, if God isn't going to answer my prayers, then I certainly can't count on the world to do it. It feels difficult; I am challenged to stay engaged in my relationship with God, and I most certainly don't want to hear what anyone has to say because none of what they have to say will change a single blessed thing. I feel defeated, worn out, stressed, angry, frustrated, and worse, I feel hopeless. I question my relationship with God in these moments and wonder where he is. I know I am not alone in this, so if you can relate to it, I promise it will improve. I tell myself this because if God has kept me breathing and upright, He has a solution already available, and I have to pray and ask to receive it. The dictionary defines hope as a feeling of expectation and desire for something to happen.

Pastor Hennie Bosman defines biblical hope as the confident expectation of God's promised future that fuels one's faith in Christ and love for others. (Hennie Bosman, 2019, www.gotrock.org)

Now, if you look at the two definitions, they seem similar. However, the one on top is the worldly and secular definition of hope. You see, we cannot simply live on a feeling. Feelings confuse the situation and often lead us to make poor decisions. It's like when someone goes to a horse race and says they feel their horse of choice will win. They place a large bet on that horse, then the horse loses. The person's feelings have let them down, and now they are out all that money they bet on the horse. We sometimes live our lives based on emotions, so we feel on an emotional rollercoaster. I have described feeling this way before, so I know what I am talking about.

Instead of going just on feelings, we must focus on biblical hope. A hope that is lasting and based on God's promises. Colossians 1: 4-5 says: "Since we heard of your faith in Christ Jesus and your love for all the saints; because of the hope, which is laid up for you in heaven, of which you heard before in the word of the truth of the gospel." Confident hope is biblical hope that can see us through the rough and challenging times in our lives.

## *What Causes Us to Lose Hope?*

Hope is a mindset; it begins in the mind and can end in the mind. We all need hope to cope with life's challenges. We need the ability to discern real hope from false hope. We all have natural hope, which often leads to disappointment because our hope is not in Christ but in worldly things and people.

What we need is supernatural hope. When your problems continue for weeks, months, or even years, your hope begins to flounder. If your hope is not in Christ or the promises of God, then you will fall flat on your face. With supernatural hope, we develop the endurance to withstand trials. We build character and a confident hope that all God has promised He will deliver. God cannot lie; if He makes a promise, He will come through, even when it seems like a long time.

We must work through the process to understand where and WHO we are. We often forget that we are God's children; as a result, we lose our confidence and begin to act as though God has forgotten us. I know I have done this on more than one occasion, and afterward, I have asked myself, "Who is your faith really in?" We need to develop an eternal hope of knowing who God is; we can place our hope in Him because we know who He is.

In the bible, even Job became depressed. He was so depressed that He related himself to an animal, an insect, and finally, an inanimate object. He was in such a low place because his problems seemed to have no end. I certainly know how this feels as I have been struggling for so long that I have become mentally and emotionally weak. Because of my hope in Christ, I am still standing upright and not gone at my own hands.

We lose perspective when our problems arise and continue for an extended period. We focus so much on the issues that we cannot see. It is like being in a storm: the rain blinds us, the wind howls, and our vision becomes impaired as the season rages on.

Have you ever looked at your problems and thought that no one else is going through what you are? I know I certainly have. We sit there having a pity party and wonder where God disappeared during our trials. We must understand that problems are temporary, and they will come at us from time to time. No one in this world is without problems; many of us think we are the only ones going through it. If you cannot solve a problem, then it is a fact you must learn to accept. Problems are temporary, so we should never try to solve those using permanent solutions. Pastor Hennie Bosman says: "If there are no problems in your life, then you are dead! Problems will come." (Hennie Bosman, 2019, www.gotrock.org)

I have found that my ongoing problems have made me bitter, angry, frustrated, and hopeless, and I have begun to believe God has forsaken me. I know that is not true because the enemy is a liar! Problems and trials should not make us bitter but make us better. We should grow through our trials, developing our relationship with Christ, building our character, and building our endurance to withstand life's challenges.

I can certainly relate to Jeremiah 15:18, where Jeremiah says: "I don't understand why my pain has no end. I don't understand why my injury is not cured or healed. Will you be like a brook that goes dry? Will you be like a spring that stops flowing?" Sometimes, I feel as though my blessings from God have dried up. Then, I must stop and look at everything I am blessed to have. My health, my children, my husband, my family, my friends, my skills, the knowledge he has given me, food, clothes, shelter, and so on. It's all about our perspective. Depending on our perspective, that determines our level of hope. If your viewpoint is negative and not God-focused, then it only goes without saying that your hope level will be below. We need sustaining, positive thinking and sustained prayer in our lives for us to cope with the reality that is our life.

I have found that many of us, including me, allow our problems to stop us. We become emotionally numb; the pain of our struggles drains our hope and tends to turn up the volume of our predicament. I mentioned Jeremiah above, but Job, too, struggled with the challenges and losses he faced. For some of us, God won't answer our prayers. In the case of Job, when he asked God to kill him, God ignored that request. Not everything we ask God for will come our way. Some things may not be all that good for us, and His answer is simply no. No means no, so we have to get over ourselves. That is not easy to do, as I can attest to having been on the receiving end of multiple unanswered prayers.

Sometimes, we cannot understand why God did not answer our prayers. We ask ourselves if it is because He does not love us the same as His other children. For instance, when we have a family member or friend who is ill or dying, we ask God to spare their lives. God doesn't, and we begin to doubt His love for us and that person we lost. God is God and will do what he sees as best. Perhaps it was that person's time to go, for they had fulfilled His purpose for them. When going through these things, we often feel it is a direct assault on our faith and hope. Perhaps it is. Maybe it is a test of our faith to see what or whom we believe in. All prayers are answered, just not in the way we may want or expect.

God is sovereign, and He will do whatever He wants no matter what. We are not God, and we must stop trying to be God. (Hebrews 3:6) We must learn to rest in the fact that God is in charge. My disobedience is because I don't like His answer, and I will not change the answer He gave. It is like when a parent tells a child no or not to do something, and they still do it anyway. That defiance against God will not make your problem disappear; honestly, I think it will only make it stick around longer. Too many of us want to live like: "I did it my way" instead of living in God's way. We want what we want, and we want it now! We have a mentality that if God doesn't give it to me, I will do what I want anyway.

Remember that some things don't always turn out the way we want. I lived that after I went to college to be an educator, and instead of obtaining the full-time teaching position I thought I would, I found myself substituting and being an Impact Teacher. I did everything right, yet obtaining that full-time teaching job was out of reach. I believed that once I received my dream job, I would live in peace and tranquility, working my way to retirement. I am no longer teaching. I told my husband there was more life behind me than what was ahead, so it was time to utilize a different strategy. Perhaps God has been saying no to the idea of my teaching in a classroom all along, and I was just too stubborn (or stupid) to get the picture. Hmmm, I wonder how that is all playing out in the mind of God. He is probably saying, "Well, I have been trying to show you something else all along, but you wanted to do what you wanted to, and I just let you." He does give us free will, after all.

## *Losing Hope When Our Expectations Go Unmet*

Have you ever begun to lose hope when everything you expected or hoped for has not come to fruition? I know my life has not turned out how I expected it to, and yes, I was losing hope, or it had drained so low that I could not see past my problems. I wondered to myself, "What now? Where do I go from here?" I found myself giving up on God, losing hope, and doubting that I had a future. It is not easy when you feel this way. You feel like you have hit bottom like a ton of bricks. Les Brown has said, "When life knocks you down, try to land on your back. Because, if you can look up, you can get up. Let your reason get you back up." (Les Brown, 1991, You Deserve)

When we are going through trials, we want to blame everyone, including God, when we should be looking in the mirror because many of our problems are self-induced. Granted, there are situations where we do not bring a problem onto ourselves, but quite often, financial woes or personal situations arise because of our decisions or bad judgment.

We need a community of godly people who will listen to us and give us sound advice or emotional and mental support. Our problem is that when good, honest, Godly people want to provide us with advice or help us find solutions, we are unwilling to hear what they say. We look for hope in all the wrong places versus trying to go to God for an answer. You lose focus when you place your hope in the wrong places or things. Some of us try to return to situations God saved us from in the first place because we see the temporary joy that may have brought us.

Hope is not found in those things or those individuals. Hope is found in Christ. We must consider embracing Christ and submitting our lives to Him. We need to be on our guard. (Luke 21:34) Allow hope to be the anchor of your soul. (Hebrews 6:17-19) Go to God for safety. We can and will gain strength from Him. You can do all things through Christ who strengthens you!

Remember Romans 8:28: "And we know that in all things God works for the good of those who love him, who have been called according to his purpose." We need to get into God's presence. We all know He is omnipresent, so when we gather with other Christians of like minds, we can manifest God's presence when we worship and praise Him. Our hope should be anchored in Christ in the manifest presence of God. When our hope is in Christ and not the world, we shall not be moved because our expectations are in Him. Our hope is not in the world and worldly things but in Christ, who died on the cross for us because He loved us so much.

Don't allow yourself to be drawn out of the presence of God when trials and challenges come your way. I have done this myself, and it did not come to any good whatsoever. Ask God to let His grace be sufficient for you. Ask Him to let His grace flood you, heal you, and give you a fresh start. We all need Jesus to save us, for we cannot save ourselves.

## *Stepping Into God's Promises*

I am believing and stepping into God's promises for my life. The Bible has over 1,000 references to the word "believe." Do you wonder why that is? I don't! Why? Well, God wants us to believe in His promises. I don't know what the future holds for me, but I trust God for His guidance, direction, lighting, and blessing my path. We must embrace an unknown future and leave it in the hands of a known God. He knows our future and only wants us to concern ourselves with today. I know that I am willing to hear what He has to say and to trust that He knows far better than me where He wants me to go. Every day is a new adventure with lessons to be learned. He is working on me continuously, and for that, I am thankful.

# Conclusion

I am finding freedom in the Word of God, and my reliance on Him has become more evident over time. My advice is to trust in God's will for your life and step into His promises. It will not be easy, particularly when things seem at a standstill. Give praise and thanks to God daily and find a quiet place to spend time with Him. In your quietness, listen to His voice as He speaks to you. Find the blessings in all things, great and small. There is always something to be thankful for, and I believe that by showing our thankfulness, gratitude, kindness, and generosity, we can grow closer to God and those we spend time with.

Remember that life has many challenges and temporary situations; you will get past them in due time. Pray through every challenge and difficult situation and build a team of people you can trust around you. Invite these individuals into your inner circle. Sometimes, we need trusted intercessors to pray and believe in and with us. Ask God to guide your choices for those individuals, particularly if you don't have many believers around you. If you are not part of a church family, find one! Many great pastors follow the bible and teach God's Word. I send God's blessings your way. I pray that He will be a consistent part of your life. I ask Him to guide you through your struggles and life challenges. I believe you and I can overcome anything the enemy sends us. I ask Him to intercede daily in our health, finances, relationships, businesses, and jobs. May you find comfort, peace, and joy in every aspect of your life. The devil is a liar, and we can trust and believe that God has given us the authority to overcome.

God bless you!

Susan

# References

1 Chronicle 16:34-35: "Oh give thanks to the LORD, for he is good; for his steadfast love

endures forever! ...

1 Chronicles 29:13: "And now we thank you, our God, and praise your glorious name."

1 Corinthians 15:3-7

1 Corinthians 3:1-23

1 John 1:9

1 John 3:22

1 Peter 1:1-13 - Gird up your loins

1 Peter 5:7-8

2 Corinthians 10:4-6

2 Corinthians 12:9-10

2 Corinthians 13:5

2 Corinthians 3:12-18

2 Corinthians 3:16-18

2 Corinthians 4:1-6

2 Corinthians 5:18

Acts 2:1-3

Acts 2:22-24

Bosman, Hennie (Pastor). The Rock Church, Temecula, CA. https://www.gotrock.org

Brown, Les. You Deserve Motivational Speech

Camp, Ted. 2017. https://www.silentwordministries.org/2017/10/19/the-story-of-the-silversmith/

Colossians 1:9-14

Colossians 2:6-7

Congreve, William. 1962. "Act in haste; you will repent in leisure."

Conlon, Carter. It's Time to Pray https://www.amazon.com/Its-Time-Pray-Changes-Everything

Deuteronomy 30:19

Deuteronomy 31:6

Ephesian 4:1

Ephesians 1:18-21

Ephesians 2:10

Ephesians 3:20

Ephesians 4:1-3

Ephesians 4:29 – Corrupt words)

Ephesians 4:32

Ephesians 5:15-16

Exodus 4:1-9 - Moses)

Ezekiel 37:1-10

Franklin, Kirk. "Smile."

Galatians 6:9

Genesis 41:50-52

Genesis 50:20

Hamer, Fannie Lou. 1962

Hebrews 11:33-34

Hebrews 12:1-2

Hebrews 12:3-4

Hebrews 3:6

Hebrews 6:17-19

Holmes, Sr., Oliver Wendell. "Some people are so heavenly-minded that they are of no earthly good."

I Chronicles 16: 28

I Corinthians 10: 31

I Corinthians 1-7

I Corinthians 4:8-17

I Corinthians Chapters 1-4

Isaiah 12:2

Isaiah 40:31

Isaiah 53:1-6

James 3:8-10 –The tongue

James 4:10

James 4:6

Jeremiah 15:18

Jeremiah 29:11

Job 1:21

Job 3:25

John 1:1-5

John 1:46

John 10:10

John 12:24

John 13: 12-17

John 13: 3-5

John 14:2

John 15:2

John 15:9-12)

John 17:20-26

John 19:23-24

John 20:14-18

John 20:29

John 8: 31-32

Judge 6:1-40

Keller, Helen

KWVE radio, 107.9 F.M.

Luke 1:30-37

Luke 1:38

Luke 1:42

Luke 11:13

Luke 21:34

Luke 22:44

Luke 8:4-15 – the parable about the Sower

Luke 9:23

Luke17:6

Malachi 3:3

Malachi 3:7

Mark 10:21

Mark 12:28-31

Mark 14:32-36

Mark 9:23

Matthew 10:15-Judgement

Matthew 10:16

Matthew 11:28

Matthew 13:32

Matthew 18:21

Matthew 18:23-35

Matthew 18-22

Matthew 20: 26-27

Matthew 20:17-19

Matthew 22:36-39

Matthew 27:51

Matthew 28:1-9

Matthew 5:23-24

Matthew 6:27

Matthew 6:6

Matthew 8:1-13 – Centurion

Matthew 9:16-17

Micah 6:8

Numbers 13

Philippians 2: 3-8

Philippians 2:13

Philippians 2:5-7

Philippians 2:8

Philippians 3:10-11

Philippians 4:6

Philippians 4:8

Proverbs 10:22

Proverbs 11:3-5

Proverbs 23:20-21

Proverbs 16

Psalm 23: 1-6

Psalm 56:3

Psalm 119:71

Psalm 139:14

Psalm 139:23-24

Psalm 34:4-6

Psalm 36:9

Psalm 37:7

Psalm 51:6

Psalm 56:3

Psalm 91:1-2

Romans 10:13

Romans 12:18

Romans 6:10-12

Romans 8:28

Romans 8:5-7

Titus 2:11-12

Tolkien, J.R.R. "Even the smallest person can change the course of the future."

Tubman, Harriet. "Never wound a snake; kill it."

Warren, Rick (Pastor). Daily Hope, former senior pastor of Saddleback Church, Author of The Purpose Driven Life (and many others)

Young, Jr., Whitney

# OTHER BOOKS BY THIS AUTHOR

**STORIES**
- CUPCAKE ISLAND: THE KIDNAPPED PRINCE (2024 REVISION COMING SOON)
- THE HIBISCUS CLUB MYSTERIES: THE MISSING NOTEBOOK (COMING SOON IN 2025)
- MAKING FAST FOOD: A CARIBBEAN-BASED CHILDREN'S STORY (COMING SOON IN 2025)
- ENCHANTED SNAKE ISLAND: THE MISSING TIARA (COMING SOON IN 2025)

**COOKBOOKS**
- CARIBBEAN MEDLEY: A COMPILATION OF CARIBBEAN-AMERICAN RECIPES
- DESSERTS AND BREAD (COMING SOON IN 2025)

**INFORMATIONAL BOOKS**
- THE COMPLETE RESUME GUIDE: LANDING THAT COVETED JOB
- CREATIVE WRITING COURSE
- CREATIVE WRITING COURSE WORKBOOK

**PUZZLE BOOKS:**
- KID'S CHRISTMAS ACTIVITY BOOK
- KID'S THANKSGIVING PUZZLE BOOK
- KID'S HALLOWEEN PUZZLE BOOK
- CHRISTMAS WORD SEARCH
- BIBLE-THEMED WORD SEARCH

- HALLOWEEN PUZZLE BOOK
- THANKSGIVING PUZZLE BOOK
- VALENTINE'S PUZZLE BOOK
- MUSIC AND INSTRUMENTS PUZZLE BOOK
- FOODS, FOODS, FOODS PUZZLE BOOK
- DOGS AND CATS PUZZLE BOOK
- FOURTH OF JULY AND SUMMER PUZZLE BOOK
- SEASONS PUZZLE BOOK
- SPORTS PUZZLE BOOK

## FOLLOW US ON:

- **FACEBOOK:**
    - MAGRAS LITERARY ENTERTAINMENT
    - THE HIBISCUS CLUB MYSTERIES
    - THE TRAVELER'S DETECTIVE AGENCY BOOKS
- **INSTAGRAM:**
    - MAGRASLITERARY
    - HIBISCUSCLUBMYSTERIES
    - TRAVELERSDETECTIVEAGENCYBOOKS
- **Amazon:**
    - Susan M. Magras-Edwards

## WRITING SERVICES:

Visit us at www.magrasliterary.com for your writing needs. You can also email us at magrasliterary@gmail.com or connect with us via our website. Please email us to receive our monthly newsletter filled with updates.

This book compiles the author's blog posts from her former website, Embracing Life. The information has been updated to the present day, but it also stays true to the struggles and experiences the author went through over a long period. It is intended to encourage and inspire others to find peace in their lives as they struggle with mental health. The author is not a health professional and encourages those struggling to seek a professional diagnosis and mental health assistance.

No part of this publication may be reproduced, stored in a retrieval system, or transmitted in any form or by any means, electronic, mechanical, digital, photocopy, recording, or otherwise - except for brief quotations in printed reviews - without the prior, written permission of the copyright owner.

ISBN: 979-8-9917974-5-0

Copyright © 2025 by Susan M. Magras-Edwards

Written by Susan Magras-Edwards

Book design and layout by Susan M. Magras-Edwards/Magras Literary Entertainment MLE (www.magrasliterary.com)

Published by Magras Literary Entertainment

Front and Back Cover Design by adapted from Canva

Printed in the USA

## Getting To Know The Author

Susan M. Edwards is a wife, mother, former educator, avid reader, writer, pet lover, and entrepreneur. She was born and raised on the island of St. Thomas, United States Virgin Islands. She now resides in sunny Southern California. She has two grown children, two daughters-in-law, two grandsons, and a vast extended family.

Susan spent many years working in the accounting field. Eventually, she became a teacher and worked for 17+ years. While she enjoyed teaching, she decided there were other ways she could teach and express her creativity and imagination without doing so in a classroom setting.

Through the years, Susan worked with many high school and college students, proofreading and editing their documents. She earned a bachelor's degree in business administration, a master's in organizational management (Human Resources), and a master's in education (Elementary Education).

Susan finally decided to publish her first book in 2019. Eventually, despite some setbacks, her book was first published in 2020, and printed copies became available in 2021. Her journey in writing continues with this and several other books, a cookbook, and multiple puzzle books. (See the list at the back of the book)